FINDING MEXICAN BUTTERFLIES

Roland H. Wauer

To order additional copies of this book, contact:
Xlibris
844-714-8691
www.Xlibris.com
Orders@Xlibris.com

Library of Congress Control Number: 2022915260
ISBN: Softcover   978-1-6698-4305-4
        Hardcover   978-1-6698-4306-1
        EBook   978-1-6698-4304-7

Print information available on the last page

Rev. date: 09/27/2022

Dedicated to Jim Brock

Every butterfly included below were actually observed and recorded by the author. All butterfly photographs that follow were taken by the author; the majority of the scenic were taken by Betty Wauer. Photos by others are so designated.

Mexico Butterfly Trip, January 2001

Our small group entered the state of Tamaulipas, Mexico at Progresso in mid-morning, and our first stop was at the Rio Corona. Our driver, Lee Ziegler, pulled his SUV off the highway and down the bank to park next to the river. Ben Basham, Charlie Gifford, and I jumped out and began a wandering search for butterflies up and down the riverbank.

Author at the Rio Sabinas

In a little more than two hours, I recorded 39 species, five of those were commonplace: Little and Mimosa Yellows, Sleepy and Tailed Oranges, and Common Mestra. But there were a number of Mexican species there as well. The most outstanding of those were **Banded Peacocks** [see photo B1 below], truly a gorgeous tropical butterfly which occurs in the United States only in extreme South Texas.

Our next stop, in mid-afternoon, was along the Rio Salinas. Since we planned on staying overnight at Cuidad Monte, not far beyond the Rio Salinas, we wandered along the stream and in the adjacent fields for the remainder of the day; we added 15 species to our trip list. Two of those were special in that they represented lifers for all of us: the tiny Elf and the Yojoa Scrub-Hairstreak.

With a wingspan less than half-an-inch, the **Elf** [see photo B2 below] is a brightly marked butterfly, all black with bright orange bands across both its forewings and hindwings and a round orange spot on the inner edge of the forewings.

Yojoa Scrub-Hairstreak [see photo B3 below], about three times larger than the Elf, is a tropical species which is considered a rare stray in the United States, found only in South Texas and southern Arizona. An early-day lepidopterist called it "White-stripe Hairstreak" for the white forewing bar. Larval foodplants include tick-clover and hibiscus.

Betty at the Rio Carona

Other butterflies recorded along the Rio Sabinas included Common Melwhite, Gray Bluemark, Ruddy Daggerwing, Mexican Blue-Satyr, and Two-spotted Prepona. The **Gray Bluemark** [see photo B4 below] was a striking butterfly, very much like the closely related Blue Metalmark that sometimes is found at Los Ebanos Preserve near Brownsville in Texas. Its larval foodplant was a mystery until recent years when a Blue Metalmark was discovered egg-lying on a fern acacia, a ground species.

On several earlier Mexico trips, during the years when my major interest was Mexican birds, prior being smitten with butterflies, Rio Corona was always a major stop when driving south into Mexico. I have long considered the Rio Corona as North America's northern-most tropical riparian habitat. The area always has produced several Mexican birds not found to the north; examples include Crane and Great Black Hawks, Pale-billed Woodpecker, Squirrel Cuckoo, and Blue-crowned Motmot. And on one occasion, while parked there overnight, the singing of a Mottled Owl kept me awake half the night.

One tropical butterfly I have always found along the Rio Corona is the **Mexican Bluewing** [see photo B5 below], a mid-sized butterfly with blue and black bands on the upperside and several contrasting white spots on the wingtips. Most often, I have found it perched on a tree trunk, where I am able to photograph it before it flies off to another tree. Although Bluewings can often be found in the US, particularly in the Lower Rio Grande Valley, seeing it in Mexico seemed to welcome me to their native homeland.

Hotel Monte

Not far south of the Rio Corona, we overnighted at Cuidad Monte, still in the state of Tamaulipas. Hotel Monte became my home away from home on many trips into Mexico. The rooms are clean and comfortable, and the hotel dinning room offers a variety of good food. The word "mante" comes from the Nahuatl language and is composed of three syllables in that language: "man", "atl" and "tetl", which mean "place of", "water" and "rock". Taken together these words mean "the place of the water in the rock" or "where the water comes out of the rock", alluding to the Monte River spring (El Salto), where the water surges forth over the rocks in the "Sierra de Cucharas."

El Salto Area

The following morning, we continued south and soon entered the state of San Luis Potosi. By mid-morning we were searching for butterflies at El Salto. This area is dominated by the Rio Monte which forms a series of spectacular falls and pools of deep green water. A secondary pool nearby, El Nacimiento, offers about the same habitat and is also a priority butterfly site.

The morning was foggy early but cleared by 10 am. In a way, the El Salto area, with its river and riverine habitat provides yet another high-quality butterfly site. One of the more common butterflies at El Salto, flying in-and-out of the vegetation and along the trails was the **Zebra Heliconian (or Longwing)** [see photo B6 below], a most distinct all-black species with bright yellow bands. Adults congregate at special roosts at night, and when feeding, they utilize trapline routes – a series of stops regularly visited. It can be commonplace throughout the Tropics, and it also is reasonably common along the Rio Grande floodplain in South Texas. It's larval foodplants include passion-flowers.

Rio Lerma at El Salto

El Salto was filled with marvelous tropical butterflies that morning. I recorded more than four dozen species which I had not already seen on our trip. Most outstanding were Barred and Yellow-angled Sulphurs, Giant White; Chained and Strophis Hairstreaks, Julia, Erato, Tiger and **Isabella's Heliconians** [see photo B7 below]; Blackened Bluewing, **Orange Banner** [see photo B8 below], Juno Silverspot, both Yellow-tailed and **Gilbert's Flashers** [see photo B9 below], and Gold-banded Aguna. Other outstanding butterflies found at El Salto included Juno Silverspot, Blomfild's Beauty, and Many-banded Daggerwing.

On one trip, I walked down-river along the riverbank for a mile or more; the flow below El Salto proper looked strong and deep. A Ringed Kingfisher flew ahead of me and few minutes later I found a Green Kingfisher fishing from a low-hanging tree branch.

After a full day of finding amazing butterflies at El Salto, we drove on to El Naranjo where we acquired overnight lodging at the Hotel del Valle. But we soon discovered that the hotel did not have hot water for showers and our night was noisy due to a rather rowdy family next door; we slept very little.

The following morning, we drove upward into a dense oak forest where we expected to find some high-country butterflies. But the area was rainy and foggy, so we returned to the lowlands where we walked along the roadway searching for butterflies. I added a Bromiliad Scrub-Hairstreak, Royal Greatstreak, Brown and Mayan Crescents, and Plain and Tailed Satyrs, to our trip list. The **Regal Greatstreak** [see photo B10 below] lived up to its name and more. What an amazing creature with its sharply defined underside pattern, green below and deep green wingtips, divided by a rose-colored band that extended into the tail with long black stringers.

After a couple hours in the lowlands, we continued our drive south, stopping on numerous occasions where the habitat looked worthwhile. That day produced more than four dozen trip butterflies. Five more species were highlights: Falcate Metalmark, Banded Patch, Blue-eyed Sailor, Malachite, and Rusty-tipped Page. The **Blue-eyed Sailor** [see photo B11 below] was exceptional. Males are golden-green with blackish bars and margins; females are brown with a broad, white median band. When egg-laying on noseburn, it is know to colonize. I had seen it once before in the Lower Grande Valley of Texas, but seeing it in Mexico, in its more "native" niche, helped me to better understand its environment requirements.

Of all those other truly outstanding butterflies, the larger **Malachite** [see photo B12 below] stands out to me as one of the most colorful of all Mexican butterflies; males are brighter than females, and they possess a slow and gliding flight. Malachites will forever more provides me with a long-lasting memory of the El Salto area. It is not only a beautiful creature, but also a wonderful representative of Mexican butterflies.

Gomez Farias

The following day found us in the little town of Gomez Farias and en route to Alta Cima, situated at the end of an eight-mile-long mountain road beyond Gomez Farias. We spent several hours in an around Gomez Farias before heading up to Alta Cima. Right away I recorded five hairstreaks: Broken-M, Zebra, Gold Bordered, Red-lined, and Red-spotted. The Gold-bordered and Red-spotted Hairstreak were lifers.

The **Red-spotted Hairstreak** [see photo B13 below] was a nervous little bug that flew about in a moist area, and it took me considerable time before it calmed down enough for me take its picture. It wasn't until later, when I viewed my photo close-up on a screen before I truly realized what a striking little hairstreak it was. Larval foodplants include lantanas.

Alta Cima

The village of Alta Cima lies within a beautiful little valley at approximately 5,500 feet elevation. The high ridge above the village to the west, locally known as Sierra de Guatemala, runs north to south for more than 30 miles; its highest points are more than 7,000 feet in elevation.

I was very familiar with Alta Cima and environs; years earlier I had camped there three nights while exploring the region for birds. And I also had gone beyond Alta Cima into the El Cielo Biosphere Preserve, an area considered the northernmost cloud forest in North America. We planned to butterfly both areas on this trip.

For two days, before moving up the mountain to El Cielo, we searched for butterflies within the Alta Cima area. Habitats varied there from river floodplain (Rio Sabinas) to open fields to heavy oak-dominated woodlands. And what a treasure we found! More than 150 butterfly species were recorded within the greater Alta Cima area. It is difficult to select one or a few to highlight because there were so many outstanding species.

A few of my favorite Alta Cima butterflies included Painted White, Boisduval's Yellow, Gray and Variable Crackers, Tiger Heliconian, Teleus Longtail, Yellow-tipped Flasher, Gold-spotted Aguna, Variable Cracker, and Sharp-banded and Violet-patched Skippers. Perhaps, my favorite was the **Tiger Heliconian** (see photo B14 below), a longwing with sharp orange bands and black wingtips with multiple white markings. Adults are known to roost in small groups, often under grass blades. Their larval foodplants are limited to passion flowers, plants that are commonplace on all the mid-elevation mountain slopes.

Although the heliconian certainly would win a beauty contest over any of the crackers, for me the **Variable Cracker** (see photo B15 below) was another of the highlight butterflies that day. It not only was a lifer but it stayed in one place, allowing me to get some good photos before it flew away. This cracker shows black eyespots ringed with blue and with white centers on the hindwings. All the crackers commonly perch head-down on tree-trunks.

Less exciting trip butterflies of interest that I recorded at Alta Cima included Dusky-blue Groundstreak, Red-crescent Scrub-Hairstreak, Clytie Ministreak, Myia Crescent, Rainforest and Whitish Satyrs, and Veined White-Skipper. We also found several dozen tiny **Silver-banded Hairstreaks** [see photo B16 below] on and about balloon vines, it's larval foodplant which were widespread on the surrounding vegetation. This little bug is one of Mexico's most appealing hairstreaks. It is mostly green on the underside with a straight, broad, silvery band (edged with red) that crosses both wings, and a broad brownish patch on the hindwing margin. Balloon vines can easily be identified by its one-inch-wide inflated seed pods.

In the morning we drove above Gomez Farias along a narrow mountain road from where we could look back into town and the terraced hillside gardens. But because the day was rainy and wet, we returned to the lowland to spend the day along the Rio Sabinas. It was a good decision because the storm in the mountains remained throughout the day.

We added about two dozen trip butterflies that day along the river and adjacent fields and woods. The most impressive of those was a **Common Morpho** [see photo B17 below], five inches from wingtip to wingtip, and with a baby-blue upperside edged with brown, and a chocolate brown underside with a series of eyespots on both the forewings and hindwings. Truly a gorgeous creature. In flight, it gave me the impression of a large blue and brown bat.

Other large butterfly species found that day in the lowlands included Red Rim, Blomfild's Beauty, Laothoe Banner, Banded Peacock, and Many-banded Daggerwing. Each, in its own way, deserves greater attention. But the intricate beauty of the Blomfild's Beauty and the great spreading wings of the Daggerwing are extra special.

Blomfild's Beauty [see photo B18 below] truly is a real beauty! The underside is a wild combination of white lines and circles against a brown to purple-brown background. The seldom seen upperside is sexually dimorphic. Males are mostly rusty with broad black wingtips crossed by three white spots. The antennae are long and have an orange tip on the otherwise black club. Beauties in the highlands are known to move into the lowlands in winter.

Although I have found **Many-banded Daggerwings** (see photo B19 below) on numerous occasions, both in Mexico and the Lower Rio Grande Valley, I have admired it each time. It is a huge, amazing creature with many broad, orange and black wing bands and black tails on the upperside. The underside is divided in two, with purplish-brown on the outer half and a paler-brown with gray bands on the outer half. Their appearance is rather bizarre with their strange shape and long tails.

The weather had cleared by the next morning and we finally began our journey up the mountain to El Cielo. In seven miles above Gomez Farias we reached a junction where we followed the narrow track for another nine miles to El Cielo, arriving at about 10am. Although the day was cloudy, we eventually had enough sunshine to search for butterflies.

Author at Alta Cima Junction

Much of road to El Cielo was too narrow to stop for butterflies, but in places where the road widened, we were able to stop, climb out of the vehicle and wander in search for butterflies. It was well worth it each time; we added a good number of trip butterflies along the roadsides. The most interesting of those included Tailed Orange, Mexican Silverspot, Spot-celled Sister, Angled Leafwing, and Anna's Eighty-eight. The showiest of the four was the **Mexican Silverspot** (see photo B20 below]. I had seen it a couple times in Texas, but seeing it in its native environment gave me considerable pleasure.

We had barely reached the El Cielo area before the storm descended on us with a fury. It continued throughout the day, so before dark we decided it was wiser to leave the higher slopes and return to the lowlands to spend what little time was still available along the Rio Sabinas.

Rio Sabinas

We spent the last few daylight hours searching for lowland butterflies along the riverbanks. We added another dozen trip bugs, including White-angled Sulphur, Mylita Crescent, Variegated Cracker, and White Peacock.

The **White Peacock** [see photo B21 below] is very different than the Banded Peacock, even though they belong to the same genus, *Anartia*. For me, the White Peacock is a more calming and charismatic bug. Seen in sunlight, it shows a lovely pattern of pale blues and whites, with small black dots. Its flight is usually slow and direct. In addition, White Peacocks are known to colonize in wet areas.

Although disappointed that we had not reached our goal of butterflying the El Cielo area, available time for our trip had run out; we headed for home. We had succeeded in recording 181 species, many of which were photographed.

Banded Peacock

Elf

Yojoa Scrub-Hairstreak

Gray Bluemark

Mexican Bluewing

Zebra Heliconian

Isabella's Heliconian

Orange Banner

Gilbert's Flasher

Regal Greatstreak

Blue-eyed Sailor

Malachite

Red-spotted Hairstreak

Tiger Heliconian

Variable Cracker

Silver-banded Hairstreak

Common Morpho

Blomfild's Beauty

Many-banded Daggerwing

Mexican Silverspot

White Peacock

Mexico Butterfly Trip, July 2001

Our group of six – Lee Ziegler, Scott Avetta, Ben Basham, Ruth Hoyt, Mike Overton, and I – gathered together at Lee's Mobile Home Park in Brownsville, Texas. At mid-morning the next day, with Lee driving his SUV, we entered Mexico at Matamoros, Tamaulipas. Our first stop was an unscheduled one at a rest stop only about 100 miles south of the border. It produced a surprising Red-spotted Patch, a species that was a lifer for us all. As we crowded around to take a photo, it flew away before I was able to get a picture. But that lifer was, for me, a positive omen of what was to come.

Rio Corona

By early afternoon, we reached the Rio Corona, an initial stop for birds and butterflies on all of my eastern Mexico trips. We spent more than three hours wandering along the river and in the adjacent fields and woodlands. I recorded more than 60 butterfly species that afternoon; several were Mexican endemics and two were lifers: Pale-spotted Leafwing and Yellow-tipped Flasher. I was particularly intrigued with the **Pale-spotted Leafwing** [see photo B22 below] in its behavior and appearance. Its upperside is blackish, except for a series of bluish forewing spots, while the underside is blue-black with a mottled appearance. Too often leafwings sit on vegetation too high to get a good photo, but my Pale-spotted Leafwing sat on a small stem at eye-level.

We spent our first night at the Hotel Hacienda Santa Engracia, about half-way between the border and Cuidad Victoria. I had never before stayed at the Santa Engracia, but it was one of Lee's favorite overnight stays when leading trips for folks interested in visiting areas in northeastern Mexico. And it was a lovely, comfortable place to overnight.

Day two was spent searching for butterflies on the Hacienda grounds and along the highway enroute to Cuidad Victoria where we stayed overnight at the Paradise Inn. A Malachite, a large colorful butterfly, greeted us as we entered the Paradise; another omen suggesting a successful trip. But we again had spent most of the day along the Rio Corona where we added another 36 trip butterflies. Although many of those were species also possible along the Lower Rio Grande Valley in Texas, several were Mexican specialties: Red-spotted, Ornython, and Polydamas Swallowtails, Red Rim, Damo Hairstreak, Mandana Metalmark, Crimson Patch, Pale-banded Crescent, Mexican Fritillary, Pavon Emperor, California and Spot-celled Sisters, Stalling's Flat, Teleus Longtail, and Brown-banded Skipper.

The **Crimson Patch** [see photo B23 below] was a gorgeous butterfly with a bright red patch in the center of each hindwing and coal black forewings with dozens of white spots. By the end of the day, it was obvious we had truly reached the area of Mexico where the majority of butterflies seldom are recorded in the United States.

Although I had previously seen Crimson Patch and Mexican Fritillary at Santa Ana National Wildlife Refuge in Texas, both seemed even brighter that day along the Rio Corona. The **Mexican Fritillary** [see photo B24 below] is one of only six fritillaries in Mexico, although there are almost three dozen frits in the United States. The appearance of the Mexican Fritillary is similar to that of the Variegated Fritillary, a more common US frit, but is paler and lacks the black-rimmed forewing bar and silver patches on the underside. Larval foodplants include damiana, passion flowers, and morning glories.

Beyond Cuidad Victoria is an extensive stretch of highway that follows the hills and valleys that offer a diversity of habitats, from arid slopes to brushlands to, not far beyond the town of El Encino, the Rio Sabinas. Although the Rio Sabinas usually is not as large as the Rio Corona, it nevertheless is always a productive stop for butterflies.

Rio Sabinas

We knew it was going to be an excellent stop when we discovered several **Common Morphos** [see photo B25 below] flying about. They looked like bright blue bats. Morphos are tropical species found mostly in South America, Central America, and southern Mexico. The name morpho means "changed" or "modified," undoubtedly due to its color in flight, bright blue on the upperside and chocolate-brown below.

Other species found along the Rio Sabinas that day included Mexican and Boisduval's Yellows, Ceraunus Blue, Eastern Tailed-Blue, Red-banded Metalmark, Pale-banded and Huestecean Crescents, Elf, White Peacock, Crimson Patch, Spot-celled Sister, Ruddy Daggerwing, Zebra Heliconian, Two-barred Flasher, Carolina Satyr, Whitened Bluewing, Florida Purplewing, White-striped and Teleus Longtails, Laviana and Turk's-cap White-Skippers, Tropical Checkered-Skipper, Delaware and White-patched Skippers, and Tropical Least Skipper.

Although I had seen **Ruddy Daggerwings** [see photo B26 below] several times before, including in South Texas, I stood still and admired that large, gorgeous creature for a full minute or more. Its upperside was orange-red with narrow brown stripes between the leading edge of the forewing and the tail area. Its large size and unusual shape quickly drew my attention. And when it took flight, it was swift and straight.

Most significant about the Rio Sabinas, perhaps, is the diversity of species all within one reasonably short stretch. For instance, I have recorded seven swallowtail species there: Broad-banded, Ornythion, Phoan, Thoas, Victoria, and Zebra swallowtails, as well as Montezuma Cattleheart. I had never before recorded so many swallowtails at one location.

Of the 154 butterfly species found along the Rio Sabinas that day, 72 represented trip butterflies. Although 72 is too many to mentioned them all here, a few of those were special in that they were either lifers or species I had rarely recorded before. Examples include Branges and Meora Hairstreaks, Loathe Banner, Silver Emperor, Whitened Bluewing, Mexican Silverdrop, Yellow-tipped Flasher, Double-spotted Owl-Butterfly, Four-spotted Longwing, Bold Mylon, Dusted Spurwing, Shining Blue-Skipper, Veined White-Skipper, Green-backed Ruby-eye, and Crystal-winged, Guava, Hiska, and Lisis skippers.

Of those, how can I not choose to illustrate the **Double-spotted Owl-Butterfly** [see photo B27 below] which I found perched on a shady tree trunk; it stayed in place allowing me to take some close-up photos. There are 14 species of owl-butterflies in Mexico, none in the United States. All are larger than the average butterfly and possess large eye-spots. They usually are found in shady sites, only rarely are they out and about during the daylight hours.

Two more, smaller bugs with very unique patterns found that day along the Rio Sabinas, included the **Small-spotted Flasher** [see photo B28 below] and **Chrystal-winged Skipper** [see photo B29 below]. Both were lifers I watched the Chrystal-winged Skipper for a considerable amount of time, undoubtedly because of its strange wing-pattern and behavior. No other spreadwing skipper can compare! I followed that fascinating skipper for a long time before I was able to photograph it well enough to illustrate its unusual wing pattern.

Late afternoon found us in Gomez Farias, a little village surrounded with corn fields and the junction of a narrow road that climbs up through dense brushland as it followed a route toward our next destination, Alta Cima.

Gomez Farias area

The area around Gomez Farias also produced a good variety of butterflies. For the almost three hours we spent searching there, I recorded more than 60 species. And I knew that number would increase exponentially if we spent more search time. But of the 60-plus species, two dozen were lifers or trip bugs. Most interesting were Aquamarine and Sito Hairstreaks, Mexican Silverspot, Dorante's Longtail, Veined White-Skipper, and Fantastic, Purple-washed and Tiny skippers.

My favorite of those was the **Mexican Silverspot** [see photo B30 below], truly a bright spot among a number of less colorful bugs. The Mexican Silverspot is a longwing butterfly closely related to heliconians. The upperside is orange with a dark-brown basal area and black-rimmed triangles along the trailing edge of the hindwings. Flight is usually swift and erratic. Larval foodplants are limited to passionflowers.

The **Aquamarine Hairstreak** [see photo B31 below] and **Fantastic Skipper** [see photo B32 below] also were lifers. To me, the hairstreak represented subtle beauty and the Fantastic Skipper possessed an unusual pattern that I took time to photograph. One look and I could understand the reason it was named "Fantastic." It was very different from all the other skippers I had seen.

Road to Alta Cima

The next day, we drove the rather steep, mountainside road to Alta Cima. It had no pull-outs where we could stop and check out our surroundings. But, once we reached the open flats at the village of Alta Cima, there was plenty of space; we wandered about that area for a couple hours before continuing on to San Jose. Our list of Alta Cima butterflies was less than expected, but we did add Esmeralda Longtail, Dusky Satyr, and Hermit and Purplish-black Skippers.

The **Esmeralda Longtail** [see photo B33 below] was a gorgeous bug with an emerald-green back that reminded me of soft velvet. The dark-brown forewings had a median band of silvery squares, a lone central spot, and a short subapical line of tiny white spots. My Esmeralda Longtail was very active, moving from one nectaring plant to another in quick fashion. It took considerable time, following it from one place to the other, before I was successful in taking its picture.

Alta Cima

We soon continued up the track to the village of San Jose; I discovered that butterfly species and numbers increased with elevation. Surprisingly, however, many of the species recorded there duplicated those found in the states: Black Swallowtail, Sleepy Orange, Yellow-angled Sulphur, Painted Lady, Mournful Duskywing, Carolina Satyr, Sachem, and Clouded, Fawn-spotted, Falcate, Sickle-winged, and Fiery skippers. At one place along the road, we stopped to photograph a puddling group of butterflies. I counted at least 65 individuals in that puddle. Butterflies often seek wet places where they can drink as well obtain needed nutrients.

Puddling butterflies

Once we got above San Jose, I was unsure about some of the butterflies I found. But from my list of those I recognized on site and those I photographed and identified later, I had encountered at least 75 species at San Jose and the immediate surroundings. And at least ten of those were lifers! Blackish and Ardy's Crescents, Cream-banded (Dusky) Emperor, Florida Purplewing, Dusty Satyr, and Gold-banded, Hermit, Mercurial, Rainbow, and Yellow-stained skippers.

The most impressive of the ten was the **Cream-banded Emperor** [see photo B34 below], truly a contrasting bug. The upperside is brownish-red, and the outer half of the forewing is black with buff diagonal bands. My Emperor apparently was a female; males show white spots near the wingtips. I learned later that all emperors utilize hackberry leaves for their larval foodplant.

Two unexpected butterflies found in the village included old friends; a **Chisos Banded-Skipper** [see photo B35 below] and a Mexican Tiger Swallowtail, both species that occur in Maderas del Carmen, the high mountain range southeast of Big Bend National Park. Although I had seen Chisos Banded-Skippers in Big Bend, it was far more numerous in the San Jose area that day. Its dark brown upperside clearly showed two gold wing bands and bright white serrated hindwing edges.

Continuing on from San Jose, we drove upward toward El Cielo, an area with habitats quite different from those at lower areas. And the roadsides there were moist with an abundance of flowering shrubs; we stopped whenever possible. I found four lifers: Mexican Cycadian and Goodson Greenstreak, Rosita Patch, and Dark Mylon.

The **Mexican Cycadian** [see photo B36 below] is a large, impressive hairstreak with an underside of bluish dots against a black background, truly an outstanding bug. Although cycadians do not occur in the United States, Mexico claims three outstanding Cycadians: Mexican, Superb, and Pale-tipped.

Following a successful day at San Jose and El Cielo, we returned to Gomez Farias for the night. And the following day, we drove the Ocampo Road for about 40 miles, stopping numerous times to look for butterflies. One stop was a woodland in an area locally known as the "Sierra de Cuchaios" where we spent a couple hours.

Ocampo Road

The Ocampo Roadway was our most productive area on the entire trip. In total, we found about three dozen trip butterflies along the Ocampo roadsides, and at least eleven of those were lifers: Costa-spotted Mimic-White, Myia Crescent, Rusty-tipped Page, Pale and Variegated Crackers, Whitish and Usitata Satyrs, Golden-headed Scallopwing, and Crab's-claw, Fantastic and Mercurial Skippers.

The **Rusty-tipped Page** [see photo B37 below] was the largest and brightest of the abundant butterflies recorded that day. I found three individuals, and each seemed more colorful than the last. Truly a remarkable creature! The upperside is sharply divided by a band of white squares that extend from the leading edge of the forewing to near the trailing edge of the hindwing. The basal portion of the wings are a rusty-brown, while the outer portion is orange. Larval foodplants include members of the Acanthaceae family.

Several of the other butterflies recorded along the Ocampo Road also represented trip bugs. Most memorable were Salome Yellow, White Angled-Sulphur, Red Rim, Tiger Mimic-Queen, Pavon Emperor, Variegated Cracker, and Mexican Longtail. My photo of the **Pavon Emperor** [see photo B38 below] is a male; females are dark brown with white median bands and gold blotches on the wingtips, much like Silver Emperors. All emperors utilize hackberries for their larval foodplants.

At the end of the day, we returned to El Naranjo where we stayed two more nights while we again visited the El Salto area. Our additional time there was extremely productive; I recorded more than 120 species. Of those, 47 were trip bugs, including the following species: Royal Greatstreak, Falcate Metalmark, Red-bordered Pixie, Red-rayed Sombermark, Black and Phoan Crescents, Rayed Sister, Silver Emperor, Gilbert's Flasher, Rainforest Satyr; Angled, Guatemalan, and Pointed leafwings; Common Spurwing; and Vacerra, Variegated, Violet-patched, and Ubiquitous skippers.

One of my all-time favorite butterflies is the little **Red-bordered Pixie** [see photo B39 below], a metalmark that utilizes guamuchil tree leaves for their larval foodplants. Once extremely rare in the United States, it has become fairly common after guamuchil trees were planted in the Lower Grande Valley of Texas. I recall one guamuchil tree at the outside of the Mission, Texas, La Quinta Motel, where I often stay while in the Valley. Adults shy away from direct sunlight, and it often took me several minutes to locate one when searching the guamuchil foliage. In flight, they typically are slow and fluttering.

After another overnight in El Naranjo, we drove the Maguey Road the next day into the highlands and into a heavy oak forest where we searched the area for butterflies. Although the majority of what we found was the same as what we had recorded the previous couple days, the higher up the mountain we got were greater numbers of species.

The first discovery was a Regal Hairstreak, and that was followed by a Ventral Blue-Skipper and two new satyrs: Two-pupil and Cissia Satyrs. And then I had my first clearwing of the trip, a **Broad-tipped Clearwing** [see photo B40 below]; its transparent wings were edged with red borders and it showed a broad, white blotch across the black wingtips. Although I have seen very few clearwings during my travels in the tropics, I have long held the belief that, more than any other group of butterflies, clearwings are the epitome of what butterflies can be expected in cool, moist areas of the tropics.

About 12 miles above El Naranjo, we discovered a Microwave Station Road to our right. We then drove up to the open area where we found a dirt track that took us to the very top of the mountain. We spent time at the Microwave Station first and then continued up the mountain.

Of 50 species found in and around at the Microwave Station grounds, seven were lifers: Mountain White, Superb or Great Cycadian, Blackish and Mayan Crescents, Asine Longtail, Bold Mylon, and Yellow-stained Skipper. I was impressed by the contrasting black-and-white pattern of the **Mayan Crescent** [see photo B41 below].

But it was the **Superb Cycadian** [see photo B42 below] which impressed me most. What an incredible butterfly it was, large for a hairstreak and with an underside pattern of numerous white and blue spots. The upperside, which is seldom exposed because it normally perches with closed wings, is deep blue-black with pale arrows facing inward and edged with white. The larval foodplants for cycadians include cycads.

The mountain top contained an additional habitat to survey for butterflies. I listed 29 species in my field journal, of which eight were trip bugs: Magnificent Swallowtail, Dusky-blue Groundstreak, Creamy Stripe-Streak, Falcate Metalmark, Mystery Sister, Orange-edged Roadside-Skipper, and Blue-studded and Sharp-banded Skippers. Five were lifers:

Magnificent Swallowtail, Creamy Stripe-Streak, Superb Cycadian, Mystery Sister, and Blue-studded Skipper.

The **Magnificent Swallowtail** [see photo B43 below] is only one of 20 swallowtails in Mexico, but it truly is one of the most magnificent. None of the others show such bright yellow bands against a coal-black background. Truly a magnificent creature!

Swallowtails are well-known for their behavior of flying upward to the mountain tops. They apparently have a greater chance of finding a mate who also fly to the mountain tops to mate.

Rio Sabinas

After another night at El Naranjo, we headed for home. We stopped at the Rio Sabinas, where we added five trip butterflies: Dark Kite-Swallowtail, Eclipsed Cross-Streak, Sealpoint Metalmark, Tailed Satyr, and Liris Skipper.

The **Dark Kite-Swallowtail** [see photo B44 below] was a lifer, and a most welcome one. The blackish-brown underside had median band across both wings, white lines between the band and leading edge of the forewing, a submarginal band of white lines, red spots on the inner edge of the hindwing, and a long black tail edged with white. It truly was a colorful swallowtail!

I had a difficult time getting a good photograph of this large butterfly; it was constantly on the move. And it seemed to prefer slow, running water, where it seemed to be dipping now and again.

We stopped again in Cuidad Victoria, where we stayed overnight at the Valle Hotel. And in the morning, we also spent three hours at the Rio Corona before heading to the border and home. Our brief stop at the Rio Corona produced three more trip bugs: Ruby-spotted Swallowtail, Giant White, and Common Buckeye.

The **Ruby-spotted Swallowtail** [see photo B45 below] was also a lifer for me. Although it does occur as a rare visitor in the Lower Rio Grande Valley in Texas, I had missed it there in spite of many trips to the Valley. The upperside of this swallowtail was coal-black except for three red oblong patches at the base of each tail which showed a few narrow white edges. Ruby-spotted Swallowtails are known as wanderers and have been recorded in several of the southern states.

Our grand total list of trip butterflies included 292 species, and such high numbers inspired me to see more. My longing for more Mexican butterflies was put on hold until my next trip in January 2002.

Pale-spotted Leafwing

Crimson Patch

Mexican Fritillary

Common Morpho

Ruddy Daggerwing

Double-spotted Owl-Butterfly

Small-spotted Flasher

Chrystal-winged Skipper

Mexican Silverspot

Aquamarine Hairstreak

Fantastic Skipper

Emerald Longtail

Cream-banded Emperor

Chisos Banded-Skipper

Mexican Cycadian

Rusty-tipped Page

Pavon Emperor

Red-bordered Pixie

Broad-tipped Clearwing

Mayan Crescent

Superb Cycadian

Magnificent Swallowtail

Dark Kite-Swallowtail

Ruby-spotted Swallowtail

Mexico Butterfly Trip, January 2002

It was six months since my last butterfly trip into Mexico, and I was anxious to see more of Mexico and its abundant butterfly fauna. So, I drove down to Brownsville, Texas to Lee Ziegler's Motor Home Court, where I met my companions. With Lee diving his SUV, our group of Ben Basham, Wanda Dameron, Joe Holman, and me (Ro Wauer), crossed the border into Tamaulipas early in the morning of January 6, and by noon we reached our first survey site at the Rio Sabinas. We spent the remainder of the day searching for butterflies along the river before going on to Cuidad Mante where we stayed overnight at the Monterrey Hotel.

Rio Sabinas

The first day along the Rio Sabinas produced a total of 69 species of butterflies, but none were lifers; I had butterflied the Rio Sabinas area on many earlier occasions. Several of the butterflies found that day, however, were Mexican species that are extremely rare or do not occur north of the border. These included, but are not limited to, Polydamas Swallowtail, Montezuma Cattleheart, Giant White, Pearly-gray and Sito Hairstreaks, Clench's Greenstreak, Mexican Cycadian, Red Rim, Malachite, Blackened Bluewing, Erato Heliconian, Teleus Longtail, and Sunrise and Ubiquitous skippers.

The most welcome butterfly of the day was a **Polydamas Swallowtail** [see photo B46 below], a large gorgeous creature, with a wingspan of about four inches. It is coal-black on the upperside with a submarginal band of golden-yellow arrows, all pointed toward the head. It sometimes is known as "Gold Rim." Like several other swallowtails, its larval foodplants are pipevines.

The **Montezuma Cattleheart** (see photo B47 below] also a swallowtail, is another large showy butterfly, and one, perhaps because of its name, receives considerable attention. The upperside of its wings is black, without a band and with one row of red crescents along the hindwing margin. It uses pipevines for its larval foodplants.

There is a second Mexican cattleheart – White-dotted Cattleheart – on the west coast. It is similar but lacks the shallow, bright red crescents on the trailing edge of the hindwings.

Early the next morning, we drove on to El Naranjo. After securing rooms at the El Naranjo Motel, we drove out to El Salto, one of my all-time favorite places. El Salto area contains a swift-running stream, locally known as the Rio Monte, that pours over cliffs to form natural pools below before continuing downstream. I have walked a mile or more below the falls, and discovered that the river floodplain supports an abundance of wildlife, especially butterflies.

El Salto

From 10am to about 4pm, we wandered about the El Salto area, searching for butterflies. I recorded about six dozen species that day. Although I had seen many of them before, such as the Banded Peacock, Mexican Bluewing, and Isabella's Heliconian, and more than a dozen species were lifers. These included Salome Yellow, Statira Sulphur, Creamy White, Tiger Mimic-White, Pale-banded Crescent, Tiger Heliconian, Dingy Purplewing, Pointed Leafwing, Ustata and Whitish Satyrs, Tailed Gemmed-Satyr, Pale Mylon, and Redundant, and Rita skippers.

I was most impressed with the **Tiger Heliconian** [see photo B48 below], and the Pointed Leafwing, both colorful species perching nearby. The Tiger Heliconian is a Tropical longwing, closely related to the Zebra Heliconian, but it is not found in the US. It looks like Isabella's Heliconian with a brighter pattern and black wingtips with large yellowish patches. And like all the heliconians, its larval foodplants are limited to passionflowers.

Some of the other butterflies of note that day at El Salto included Orange-barred Sulphur, Dusky-blue Groundstreak, Gray Ministreak, Isabella's Heliconian, Mexican Silverspot, Banded Peacock, Orange Banner, Pearly Leafwing, Spot-celled Sister, Ruddy Daggerwing, Two-eyed Sailor, Yellow-tipped Flasher, Nabokov's Satyr, Chisos Banded-Skipper, and Fawn-spotted Skipper.

We spent the night in El Naranjo at the del Valle Hotel, and the next morning we drove up the Microwave Station Road into oak habitat. We thought we might have good luck in a different habitat, but we added very few new trip bugs that day. Exceptions included Mexican Dartwhite, Spring Azure, American and Painted Ladies, American Snout, and Sachem. It was pretty much a busted day!

The **Mexican Dartwhite** [see photo B49] had been one of my most elusive species over the years. It has been recorded in Big Bend National Park in Texas, and in spite of the many years I worked in the park, I never was able to see it there. Although I had recorded it on previous Mexico butterfly trips, I had been unable to get good photos until today. One interesting fact about this species is that its larval foodplants are mistletoes that grow on trees. Males patrol back and forth along linear pathways and deep canyons. Flight is usually well above the ground.

The next morning, after another night in El Naranjo, we drove back to the El Salto area, arriving there in mid-morning. And during the next several hours searching for butterflies, I recorded a total of 66 species. Many were the same as those recorded earlier, but I did add 30 additional species to our trip list. Resurveys of suitable areas often demonstrate what an area might offer if time permits.

Most interesting of the new species were Gold-bordered Hairstreak, White Scrub-Hairstreak, Falcate Metalmark, Clytie Ministreak, Ardy's Crescent, Red Cracker, Common Banner, Salenas False-Skipper, Gold-headed Bolla, and Chocolate-brown, Delaware, Portrillo, Purple-washed, Sharp-banded, and Violet-banded skippers. The well-marked hairstreaks – Golden-bordered Hairstreak and White Scrub-Hairstreak – also attracted my attention, and I was able to photograph both species.

The **Common Banner** [see photo B50 below] was extremely showy, and I spend considerable time before getting a photograph that highlighted its contrasting colors. The underside of the Common Banner is primarily brown with a wide goldish band across the forewing. Some authors refer to this tropical species as "Dimorphic Bark Wing," due to its cryptic underwing pattern. This is another of Mexico's tropical butterflies that has been recorded in South Texas in fall. Its larval foodplants include soapberry vines.

Alta Cima roadway

After another night in El Naranjo, we drove up to Alta Cima where we spent less than two hours before realizing that the area, for some reason, was dead. There were very few butterflies moving about, although I did record a **Superb Cycadian** [see photo B51 below], a truly amazing creature with an underside dominated by blue and pale spots scattered overall and against a coal-black background. It differs from the Mexican Cycadian by the number and distribution of spots; the spots on the undersides of Mexican Cycadians occur only on the trailing portions of the wings.

Our visit to Gomez Farias was little more than a quick check before going back to the Rio Sabinas, where we had such good luck the day before. We arrived there a little after the noon hour and spent about four hours before continuing on to El Naranjo for the night. While checking the El Naranjo grounds before dark, I found four additional lifers: Ghost Yellow, Tile White, Apricot Sulphur, and Black-patched Bluemark.

The **Black-patched Bluemark** [see photo B52 below] was especially appealing. It reminded me of Blue Metalmarks that I have seen in the Lower Rio Grande Valley at the Los Ebanos Preserve. Like Blue Metalmarks, Black-patched Bluemarks are sexually dimorphic; males are bright blue and females are orange-brown.

The majority of the butterflies found at Gomez Farias were repeats, although there were three exceptions: Red-rayed Sombermark, Tropical Leafwing, and an Interrupted Longtail. Both the Red-rayed Sombermark and Interrupted Longtail were lifers. The **Red-rayed Sombermark** [see photo B53 below], a tropical metalmark, contains median and a submarginal red band, a black dot between the two bands, and a red tail-patch on its underside. The upperside, which is seldom seen, is mostly an overall brown with a broad red stripe on the inner portion of the hindwing.

The **Interrupted Longtail** [see photo B54 below], refers to the dark interrupted bands on the underside of its hindwings. The underside or the forewings contain three separate lines of white squares, and its tail is reasonably short and black. Another unusual marking is a white circle above the eyes. Mexico has more that three dozen long-tailed skippers, and I had seen many of them in the past; Interrupted Longtail, however, was a most welcome lifer.

Casa de Piedras at Gomez Farias

For the next two days we stayed at Gomez Farias, overnighting at the Casa de Piedras and spending our daylight hours within the Rio Sabinas area. Once again, I found that the Rio Sabinas area possessed marvelous butterfly habitats. Besides the river floodplain and adjacent woodlands, the area offers open fields and urban settings. I recorded more than 130 species there all together; 35 were trip butterflies; 9 were lifers: Dina Yellow, Dusky Sombermark, Tropical Buckeye, Glaucous Cracker, Frosty-tipped Clearwing, Gilbert's Flasher, Four-spotted Longtail, Obscure Bolla, and Shining Blue-Skipper.

Gilbert's Flasher [see photo B55 below] grabbed my attention early-on; its two-toned colors, a dark blue on the forewings near the body, and chocolate-brown elsewhere. It lacks any white streaks or bars. It contrasted with the bright green foliage. And the way it moved seemed to demand a photo. Once again it took some time to acquire just the right photograph. Mexico has about two dozen flashers, and they all seem nervous as they move about.

We had spent six days in some marvelous Mexican butterfly country in January 2002; I recorded a total of 203 species. Many of those were lifers, and all provided marvelous memories.

Polydamas Swallowtail

Montezuma Cattleheart

Tiger Heliconian;

Mexican Dartwhite

Common Banner

Superb Cycadian

Black-patched Bluemark

Red-rayed Sombermark

Interrupted Longtail

Gilbert's Flasher

Mexico Butterfly Trip, January 2004

Three of us - Ben Basham, Joe Holman, and I – met in Brownsville at Lee Ziegler's Motor Home Court on January 7, and the following day we boarded Lee's SUV and crossed the border into Tamaulipas, Mexico. Our route that day took us through San Fernando, across the Rio Parificacion, through Cuidad Victoria, to Cuidad Mante, located near the border with the state of San Luis Potosi. By early afternoon we arrived at El Nacimiento, just north of Cuidad Mante, and began our search for butterflies.

Almost immediately, I recorded several Zebra Heliconians and a Brown Longtail. Although Zebras are commonplace in much of Mexico, they even reach South Texas. The **Brown Longtail** [see photo B56 below] has a much smaller range, primarily along the Gulf and West Coasts. It also occurs irregularly in south Texas where I recorded it at Santa Ana National Wildlife Refuge. Most longtails possess lines or blotches on their uppersides, but Brown Longtails are overall brown, lacking any obvious markings.

El Naciemento

We spent the remainder of the afternoon searching for butterflies at El Naciemento on the Rio Mante, a large area of pools and riparian vegetation, but it also is a popular recreation area for local families. In spite of the human traffic, I recorded 56 butterfly species there. Some of the more impressive Mexican species included Erato, Julia, and Orange-banded heliconians; White Peacock, Ardy's Crescent, Malachite, Common Morpho, Common Banner, Red Rim, Glaucous Cracker, and Large Spurwing.

The **Malachite** [see photo B57 below] was a magnificent creature; one of Mexico's most impressive butterflies. The upperside contains a patchwork of greenish patches across both wings, two square patches on the wingtips, and a series of yellow oblong dots on the trailing edge, all against a brown background. The underside contains greens and browns that are crossed by a median band. No other butterfly could possibly be confused with a Malachite. Although my Malachite was perched on a large green leaf, they often are found at ground level feeding on overripe fruit, especially mangoes and bananas. Malachites occur throughout the tropics, and also are found irregularly in the United States in the Lower Rio Grande Valley of Texas.

Several other Nacimiento butterflies also were amazing. It took me considerable time to get a good photo of a **Large Spurwing** [see photo B58 below], the next butterfly I had the privilege to photograph. I had to find just the right angle so that all its features were visible. Its' pattern of brown and black patches help to camouflage this large butterfly when it sits in the open. The spurwing name comes from the short spur-like projections on the outer edge of the lower wings.

Hotel Mante

The following day, after an overnight at Hotel Mante, we drove to El Salto, one of my favorite butterfly sites that I described in an earlier chapter. All that day and the next morning, we searched the El Salto area for butterflies. I recorded more than 60 species, although none were lifers. But several were special in that they represented Mexican species I seldom see.

That group of butterflies included Statira, Falcate Metalmark, Pale-banded Crescent, Guatemalan Tegosa, Yellow-tailed Flasher, Gold-spotted Aguna, and Redundant and Variegated Skippers. **Variegated Skipper** [see photo B59 below] is a tiny spread-winged skipper often overlooked due to its small size, wing patterns, and its behavior of sitting with wings folded downward. It blends in extremely well with its surroundings.

El Salto

The following day found us back at El Salto. No matter how many times I have searched that area for butterflies, more are still possible. One of the first species found that day was a **Ruddy Daggerwing** [see photo B60 below] that was feeding on papaya flowers. This is a huge brilliant orange creature with three dark stripes against an orange background and long, stubby tails.

I also photographed an **Anna's 88** [see photo B61 below] that perched on Joe's arm. It probably found some salt there and seemed calm, allowing us all to take multiple photos.

The remainder of the day proved my point that there was much more to be found at El Salto. The most impressive additional finds that day included Great Southern White, Marias Hairstreak, Mandana Metalmark, Silver Emperor, Red Rim, Juno and Mexican Silverspots, Isabella's Heliconian, Rosita and Crimson Patches, Two-eyed Sailor, Broad-tipped Clearwing, Gray Cracker, Rainforest and Whitish Satyrs, Two-barred and Yellow-tipped Flashers, Tanna Longtail, and Gold-spotted Aguna. Less impressive butterflies, but nevertheless new trip bugs found, included Fatal and Falcate Metalmarks, Pale-banded Crescent, and Falcate and Portrillo Skippers.

Finding a clearwing is always serendipitous, and this **Broad-tipped Clearwing** [see photo B62 below] was a lifer. I get truly excited when finding a clearwing. There is something very tropical about clearwings, reminding me at the time that I truly am in the Mexican tropics, not the United States. A Broad-tipped Clearwing has the obvious features of clearwings: broad rounded wings with windows where, in the right light, you actually can see through. And the Broad-tipped Clearwing, unlike most of the others, features broad black wingtips and a long, broad white smudge across the upper wings.

The **Silver Emperor** [see photo B63 below] was also special. I had not recorded it on earlier visits to El Salto, but now I was able to admire it at leisure. This was a female with silvery undersides, broad white median bands above and a large yellow square near the wingtips; males show a greater amount of yellow toward the wingtips. Both are stub-tailed.

The next morning we drove up to El Naranjo, but we did not stay long. The weather was cold and rainy, and it did not appear to be clearing anytime soon. By 10:30am, therefore, we were back in the lowlands along the Rio Sabinas. Although the majority of the butterflies found there were repeats of what I had already recorded, I did add a dozen trip bugs: Yellow Angled Sulphur, Lyside, Fatal Metalmark, Queen, Soldier, Snout, Dingy Purplewing, Rainforest and Tailed Satyrs, Teleus Longtail, and Myi and Purplish-black Skippers.

I was especially intrigued with the **Dingy Purplewing** [see photo B64 below]. It was sitting on a large rock which Ben had painted with a special brew he had brought from home. His brew is a concoction of bananas, beer, and brown sugar. To make a big batch, here is the receipt: 1. Place a dozen or more overripe bananas in a large blender (it may be necessary to user two or more blenders). 2. Add one-half pound of brown sugar. 3. Add one-half bottle of beer; consider how strong it might be necessary; if it is to be painted on a post or tree it should be thicker than if it is used on a flat surface. Once mixed, place it in a container and place the container in the sun for a couple of days. Be sure that the container lid is loose or the container could "blow up." Your bait is ready!

Whenever I have used that brew, it has worked extremely well; it seems to attract many of the larger butterflies. The Dingy Purplewing is but one example.

Of the dozen trip bugs found along the Rio Sabinas, the **Tailed Gemmed-Satyr** [see photo B65 below] represented a new species from an area I had visited many times. Although I had seen it in my earlier travels in Mexico, it was new for the Rio Sabinas. I include it here in spite of the photo showing a damaged hindwing.

Village of Alta Cima

The following day we drove to Alta Cima, where the weather was cooperative. I recorded more than 40 butterflies that day. Although most were repeats, several were trip bugs: Salome Yellow, Florida White, Sito Hairstreak, Stained Greenstreak, Mexican Azure, Texan Crescent, and Crab's-claw, Pasture, and Remus skippers.

The **Florida White** [see photo B66 below] seemed almost out of place among the numerous more brightly colored butterflies. However, its wings seemed to glow a satiny white, with the sunlight against its very black body. And there was a tiny yellow patch on the wing base. Although I had previously seen this butterfly within the Lower Rio Grande Valley in South Texas, it represented a new Mexican bug for me.

We overnighted at Mante, and the next morning we decided to visit a nearby canyon area, locally known as Canon La Libertad. And what a marvelous place it was! I had never visited the site before and after my first butterfly sighting, I knew it was going to be a good butterfly-day.

Canon La Libertad

From 11am to late afternoon, I recorded 68 species; 25 were trip bugs: Painted White, Dina Yellow, Gray and Pearly-gray Hairstreaks, Creamy Stripe-streak, Marine Blue, Pearl Crescent, Band-celled Sister, Common Banner, Red Rim, Cream-banded Dusky Emperor, Blomfild's Beauty, Blackened Bluewing, Gray and Guatemalan Crackers, Pale-spotted Leafwing, Dorantes Longtail, Dark Mylon, Glazed Pellicia, Texas Powdered-Skipper, Pale Sicklewing, and Hoary, Long-tailed, and White-patched skippers.

Perhaps it was the **Band-celled Sister** [see photo B67 below] that I gave the most attention to. There are more than 30 Sisters in Mexico, and there are only two Sisters in the U.S.: California and Band-celled Sisters. Finding this Band-celled Sister on our last day in Mexico was a perfect ending to our trip.

The next day we headed home. It had been a super trip with 164 butterfly species recorded. Our success made me anxious to return to Mexican butterflies as soon as possible.

Brown Longtail

Malachite

Large Spurwing

Variegated Skipper

Ruddy Daggerwing

Anna's 88

Broad-tipped Clearwing

Silver Emperor

Dingy Purplewing

Tailed Gemmed-Satyr

Florida White

Band-celled Sister

Mexico Butterfly Trip, October 2004

Frank Hedges, Derek Michalak, and I left Mission, Texas, where we had been attending the annual meeting of the North American Butterfly Association (NABA), in the early morning of October 19. By noon we arrived at Los Trancones in central Tamaulipas, Mexico. An entrance sign over the road read: "Parque Ecologico Los Trancones." And yet, we discovered early-on that the area also was a popular place for the locals to recreate.

Entrance to park

We piled out of our vehicle, stretched our legs, and began searching for Mexican butterflies. Although much of the immediate area was trampled down, the vegetation above the roadsides and adjacent hillsides were covered with brush. Almost immediately I discovered a **Black Hairstreak** [see photo B68 below], a lifer and a most welcome species. This is a drab little butterfly with several pale median lines, pale edges, and an antenna with a gold tip. I believed that finding that first lifer was a good omen for the rest of the trip.

Very soon we began wandering up-canyon along the Rio Los Trancones, and we discovered that the area contained a rich diversity of butterflies. The further up-canyon we went the greater the diversity. My partial-day total amounted to 112 species, including, in addition to the Black Hairstreak, 12 more lifers: Band-gapped or Torquata Swallowtail, Palid-tile White, Creamy Stripe-Streak, Clench's Greenstreak, Walker's Metalmark, Four-spotted Sailor, Turquoise Emperor, Frosted Flasher, Guatemalan Leafwing, White-crescent Longtail, and Bruised and Elegant skippers.

Of those dozen species, the **Band-gapped Swallowtail** [see photo B69 below] was the most exciting. It took me almost a half-hour, following it along the stream before I was able to acquire a usable photograph. The band-gapped name is derived from the separate yellow bands near the wingtips separated from the broad, median yellow bands. The Torquata name is a Latin word meaning "adorned with a neck chain or collar." My photo, however, does not show that feature.

In addition, a **Frosted Flasher** [see photo B70 below] attracted my attention by its behavior of making quick moves (or flashing). The species name is derived from the broad frosty-white margin on the underside. It rarely was still but moved here and there as if was not satisfied with its current position. I took me several minutes before it was still enough for me to photograph it. Truly a unique bug!

Several other butterflies found at Los Trancones were especially appealing. Although it is impossible to include all of them in this short dissertation, I will mention several: Ruby-spotted and Ornython Swallowtails, Montezuma Cattleheart, Pearly-gray Hairstreak, Red-crescent Scrub-Hairstreak, Blue Metalmark, Chestnut and Pale-banded Crescents, Pavon Emperor, Ruddy Daggerwing, Common Banner, Four-spotted Sailor, Red Rim, Malachite, Dingy Purplewing, Broken Silverdrop, Two-barred Flasher, and Glaucous and **Red Cracker** [see photo B71 below].

Crackers are always a surprise to me; unless they move from one tree trunk to another, finding one is a little serendipitous. The cracker name is derived from the surprisingly loud cracker sound they make in flight. There are twelve species of crackers in Mexico, four in the United States. **Gray Cracker** [see photo B72 below] is the most common cracker in much of the tropics and it barely reaches the Lower Grande Valley in Texas; the exception is one that turned up in my yard when living near Victoria, Texas. About 400 miles north of Los Trancones.

Los Trancones

Banded Peacocks [see photo B73 below] were surprisingly common that day at Los Troncones. Although I had seen it before in Mexico, I had never seen the numbers that were present at Los Troncones that day. Walking along the river, I found more than two dozen within a very short distance. Banded Peacocks fly with quick wingbeats and short glides. And they "avidly visits flowers;" their foodplants include members of the Acanthus family, widespread in both Mexico and the United States.

We spent our first night in Cuidad Victoria at the Hotel Vista Verde. And the next morning we drove to El Novilla Canyon, very close to Cuidad Victoria. It was a new site for me although I had been in and around Cuidad Victoria on several earlier occasions.

Author in El Novilla Canyon

El Novilla Canyon presented a very different combination of habitats and butterflies than any of the other sites visited on this trip. From 8am to 3pm, I recorded 36 trip butterflies, but only three were lifers: Tropical Greenstreak, Elegant Flat, and Red-studded Skipper. The **Red-studded Skipper** [see photo B74 below] seemed to be waiting for me to photograph it; it was perched atop a white daisy in the open and was very patience while I maneuvered about to take its picture.

Several of the other butterflies at El Novillo also were special. They included Tropical Greenstreak, Brilliant Greenmark, Cyna Blue, Square-tipped Crescent, Rusty-tipped Page, Band-celled Sister, Tailed Aguna, False Duskywing, Tropical Least skippers, and Gold-washed and Orange-spotted Skippers.

Orange-spotted Skipper [see photo B75 below], with a wingspan about one inch, is one of my all-time favorite butterflies. It is rarely found in open areas, preferring quiet niches, especially along streams. I did not see it at first, but once I found one, I discovered several more in the moist area next to the stream.

In mid-afternoon we returned to Los Troncones for the last two hours of the day. In that short time, I added 14 trip butterflies. Most memorable were a Dark Kite-Swallowtail, Green-backed Ruby-eye, Superb Cycadian, Erato Heliconian, Juno Silverspot, Gilbert's Flasher, Florida Purple, Zilpa Longtail, and Delicious Skipper.

I was extremely impressed with the **Superb Cycadian** [see photo B76 below], a large hairstreak without the usually hairstreak tails but with an underside filled with numerous spots, including a few blue ones, all against a coal-black background. And on a closer look I could see that its black head contained faint yellowish eye marks. It truly was a superb creature!

During our five-day wanderings, I recorded 172 butterfly species. Many of those were marvelous examples of what Mexican butterflying is all about. Every turn, every niche, and every day is likely to produce another amazing butterfly.

Black Hairstreak

Band-gapped Swallowtail

Frosted Flasher

Red Cracker

Gray Cracker

Banded Peacock

Red-studded Skipper

Orange-spotted Skipper

Superb Cycadian

Mexico Butterfly Trip – January 2005

Ben Basham, Janet Rathjan, and I met at Lee Ziegler's Mobile Home Park in Brownsville, Texas, on January 5. The next day, with Lee driving his SUV, we reached the Rio Sabinas, Tamaulipas, by late morning. Although I had spent considerable time along the Rio Sabinas in the past, I knew that there was much more to find. We immediately began our search for butterflies.

Rio Sabinas

During the remainder of the day, I recorded 40 butterfly species. Most interesting were Common Melwhite, Barred Yellow, Pale-banded Crescent, Banded and White Peacocks, Common Spurwing, Golden-headed and Mazans Scallopwings, Veined White-Skipper, and Fawn-spotted and Portillo Skippers. The **Golden-headed Scallopwing** [see photo B77 below] attracted my attention first; its head and palpi were bright yellow and it sat still allowing me to get several photographs. On a closer look, its upperside was blackish-brown with two tiny, white subapical spots; the scalloped fringes were barely evident. Some authors refer to this bug as "Ceos Skipper," after its scientific species name. Adults utilize pigweeds for their larval foodplant.

Our first overnight was spent at the Paradise Inn in Cuidad Victoria, well situated for visiting several nearby butterfly sites. In the morning we drove to Poza Azul, a beautiful ponded area on the Rio Azul, via a four-mile unmaintained roadway. But it was worth the trip. I recorded one lifer and 27 trip butterflies there, including White and Yojoa Scrub-Hairstreaks, Rounded Metalmark, Whitened Bluewing, Tropical Leafwing, Gemmed Satyr, and Laviana White-Skipper.

The **Whitened Bluewing** [see photo B78 below] was the bug of the day, and I got excited when I realized that it also was a lifer. But my photo (below) looks rather odd because of how the available light give it a two-tone appearance. It closely resembled a faded Mexican Bluewing, but the blue wing bands are club-shaped rather feather shaped. A small difference!

By 4pm we were back at the Rio Sabinas, where we butterflied for a couple more hours. I added only three trip butterflies: Mimosa Yellow and Redundant and Violet-patched Skippers. We then drove back to Cuidad Victoria for the night.

The next morning, we returned to the Rio Sabinas for a brief period, where I added a Dina Yellow and a Falcate Skipper, before continuing on to Gomez Farias where we stayed overnight. Gomez Farias is a neat little town with less than 1000 inhabitants, and it is located in the foothills from where one can see much of the surrounding countryside. I have always felt comfortable in Gomez Farias. Accommodations are nothing special but very adequate.

That afternoon we spent a couple hours searching for butterflies in the Gomez Farias area before settling in for the night. I added three trip bugs: Mexican Yellow, Cyna Blue, and Mazans Scallopwing, but none were lifers.

La Florida

The next morning, we drove to La Florida, a beautiful riverine area surrounding by lots of good natural habitat. Although I recorded less than two dozen species there, nine were trip bugs and two – Painted White and Tiger Heliconian - were lifers. Other species of interest included: Ghost White, Mimosa Yellow, Mexican Bluewing, Dingy Purplewing, and Turk's-cap White-Skipper.

The showiest was the **Tiger Heliconian** [see photo B79 below]. Although it looks very much like Isabella's Heliconian, it differs by a brighter appearance with white spots, rather than orangish spots on the outer portion of its forewings. Although, I was very familiar with Isabella's Heliconians from elsewhere, the Tiger Heliconian was a lifer that morning at La Florida.

El Salto

After another night at Gomez Farias, we drove to El Salto. The day was clear and bright and temperatures were just right for butterflies and human beings. It was a super butterfly day! I recorded over 75 species of which 32 were new for the trip. I was most excited about the Giant White, Gold-bordered Hairstreak, White Scrub-Hairstreak, Juno Silverspot, Yellow-tipped Flasher, Red Rim, Frosty-tipped Clearwing, Tiger Leafwing, Nabokov's and Whitish Satyrs, Coyote Cloudywing, Turk's-cap White-Skipper, and Purple-patched Skipper. Plus, I discovered a Giant-Skipper that I was unable to identify before it flew away.

The **Red Rim** (see photo B80 below) attracted most of my attention; it truly is an outstanding butterfly. I had not recorded it at El Salto on previous trips. The Red Rim is closely related to Admirals, Banners, and several other colorful bugs. But no other Mexican butterfly possess a red rim against a black background on the upperside, while the red rim is pinkish on the underside. From either side, it is unmistakable.

The other butterfly that caught my attention that day was the **Gold-bordered Hairstreak** [see photo B81 below]. It has a very distinct pattern and can sometimes be missed. But the light was just right, and this individual hairstreak was most cooperative. Hairstreaks are fairly common throughout North America. Jeffery Glassberg lists about 150 species in his book: *Butterflies of Mexico and Central America*. Jim Brock, in *Field Guide to Butterflies of North America*, lists only 52 species.

One other hairstreak grabbed my attention that day, but I had a difficult time getting a good photo, was the **Zebra Cross-streak** [see photo B82 below]. Although there are several zebra-striped hairstreaks in Mexico, none of the others show such broad white bands against a dark-brown background. In addition, this cross-streak shows an orange head and a solid-orange tail. Its contrasting appearance is truly appealing.

Los Troncones

That night we stayed in Cuidad Victoria at the Paradise Inn, and by 10:30 the following morning we were back at Los Trancones. Although we headed north and home by early afternoon, our second visit to Los Trancones produced almost 60 butterfly species; 24 were trip bugs. And several were species I have seen only once or a few times: White Angled-Sulphur, Spot-celled & Band-celled Sisters, Blue-eyed Sailor, Mexican Silverspot, Glazed Pellicia, Pale-spotted Leafwing, Pale Sicklewing, Dark Mylon, and Hoary and Variegated Skippers. And one – Orange Banner – was a lifer!

The **Orange Banner** [see photo B83 below] held my attention for a considerable time while photographing it from various angles. The upperside is all orange-color with hardly noticeable falcated wingtips, and the underside shows large black wingtips. It truly is an impressive butterfly!

Most of Mexico's seven banners are more strongly marked with broad, bright yellow-orange and black bands. Orange and Little Banners are the exceptions.

It was time to head home, but this four-day trip had been very successful. I had recorded 124 butterfly species, of which the Orange Banner was the most outstanding and represented a lifer.

Golden-snouted Scallopwing

Whitened Bluewing

Tiger Heliconian

Red Rim

Gold-banded Hairstreak

Zebra Cross-streak

Orange Banner

Mexico Butterfly Trip, May 2006

Our destination was the Maderas del Carmen, the high mountains in northern Mexico, southeast of Big Bend National Park, Texas. The trip began when Betty and I drove to Del Rio, Texas, where we met Eric and Sally Finkelstein. After a short visit about our upcoming trip, Betty and I got a room at the Del Rio Motel 6. We had dinner at Applebee's where Jim Brock and Bob Behrstock joined us.

Pilares

The next morning, Betty, Bob, Jim and I ate breakfast at I-Hop. Afterwards we met the Finkelsteins at their home where we loaded into Eric's SUV and headed south. We stopped for lunch at Sabinal and arrived at Pilares in early afternoon where Bonnie McKinney welcomed us. Pilares is the headquarters for the Sierra del Carmen Biosphere Reserve. Bonnie is the area manager and has been a friend of mine for many years. She studied Peregrine Falcons while I was at Big Bend National Park, and we have kept in touch ever since. Bonnie also is the author of *In the Shadow of the Carmens* which includes marvelous details about the Carmen highlands.

To provide additional geographical understanding of the area, the Carmens run for about 100 miles south into Mexico; the northern end forms the eastern edge of Big Bend National Park.

Wikipedia includes the following:

> The isolation of the Sierra del Carmen and its relatively undisturbed environment has led to conservation efforts in Mexico and jointly with the United States. Much of the Sierra del Carmen has been declared by the government of Mexico the Maderas del Carmen Flora and Fauna Protected Area, a designation which allows many economic activities and private land holdings to continue to exist within the boundaries. The protected area comprises 519,730 acres. The Maderas del Carmen is part of a bi-lateral conservation project called the El Carmen—Big Bend Conservation Corridor Initiative which includes contiguous land designated for conservation on both sides of the border totaling more than three thousand acres. In 2005, Maderas del Carmen became the first designated Wilderness area in Latin America.

> The Maderas del Carmen Protected Area was created in 1994, although conservation efforts were initially slowed because the land was privately owned, either in large ranches or in the collective farms called ejidos. In 2000 a Mexican corporation, Cementos de Mexico (CEMEX) began to purchase lands for conservation in the region. On CEMEX lands livestock and fences were removed and native vegetation encouraged. By 2006, CEMEX owned 195,080 acres in or near the Maderas del Carmen and managed another 62,530 acres nearby.

Aerial of Carmens

From Pilares, we drove into the Carmen highlands to Canon Uno and a lodge where we were allowed to stay. David Padillo, the lodge manager, met us there and served as our cook all during our stay. The lodge is a marvelous structure with a large open area on the ground floor and a number of bedrooms on the first and second floors. Each of us had our own room and we ate breakfast and dinner together. Plus, David and his wife provided sandwiches and drinks when we were in the field. We were well taken care of.

Lodge

The first morning we walked back along the entrance road for about two miles to see what butterflies we could find. I located 51 species that first day; Betty got five lifers. One of my lifers was a **Short-tailed Skipper** [see photo B84 below] which got Jim very excited; it was his first Mexican record.

The majority of the butterflies found that day, however, were pretty much the same which occur within the Texas Big Bend Country, although a few of the Carmen representative species are seldom seen north of the border. Examples include Mexican Swallowtail, Thicket Hairstreak, Gray Ministreak, Canyonland and Red Satyrs, Chisos Skipperling, and Arizona, Gold-banded, Taxiles, and Umber skippers.

I was surprised at finding **Taxiles Skipper** [see photo B85 below] and **Umber Skipper** [see photo B86 below] in such large numbers. Yet, both are extremely rare in the Chisos Mountains, only 60 to 70 miles northwest of the Carmens. I also found it interesting that the majority of the Carmen butterflies were feeding on the flowers of white horehound. A member of the mint family, horehound is not native to North America, although it is widely naturalized in both North and South America.

After our morning walk, we returned to the lodge where David and his wife served us lunch. Afterwards, we walked the Oso Creek drainage searching for whatever butterflies might be presence; I recorded 42 species. The most numerous bugs were Marine and Reakirt's Blues. Species of interest also included both Two-tailed and Mexican Swallowtails, Rawson's Metalmark, Arizona Sister, Canyonland and Red Satyrs, Pacuvius Duskywing, Arizona Skipper, and Chisos and Golden Banded-Skippers.

I found that the **Red Satyr** [see photo B87 below] seemed to pose for pictures. It was especially bright; the eyespots on both the forewing and hindwings seemed to standout extremely well. Although I had seen Red Satyrs in the Chisos Mountains on several occasions, I wondered if my del Carmen satyr, because of its brighter appearance, was possibly a different form.

Oso Creek, although mostly dry on this visit, can run full after heavy rains. Bonnie described Oso Creek thusly:

> Starting high in the Carmens above Campo Dos, and continuing even higher toward Campo Tres where these canyons fork, is the beginning of Canon el Oso, so named for the many black bears that inhabit this area. It is a long winding canyon of consummate scenic beauty...There is a mountain stream with hundreds of mini-waterfalls that rush downward to Camp Uno.

Canon Oso

On one of my earlier Carmens visit, a couple friends (Grainger Hunt and friend) and I hiked the full length of Oso Creek, and took advantage of the deep pools along the way. We discarded our sweaty clothes and jumped in. The water was icy cold at first, but on a warm summer day those pools were a godsend.

The following day we drove to Dos and beyond to a parking area from where we walked to an overlook. To the northeast we could see Pico Centenera, the pointed peak visible from the Deadhorse Mountains in Big Bend. Below us and to the southeast were a series of ridges and canyons. Directly in front, below the escarpment and on to the horizon, was desert.

View northward

We returned to the lodge in late afternoon and spent the evening having dinner and visiting with Bonnie and Johnna Padilla, Bonnie's assistant. It was then when we learned about their recent discovery of a new butterfly (previously unknown); we spent a couple hours in deep conversation before turning in for the night. Johnna had showed us a specimen of his new satyr and we, especially Jim, got all excited and we planned tomorrow to find that new satyr.

Eric Finkelstein, Jim Brock (kneeling), author, and Bob Behrstock at Jaboni Satyr site

The next day, after breakfast, we drove out to the place where Johnna had collected the new bug, which they had named "Jobani Satyr," a combination of Johnna and Bonnie: **Jobani Satyr** [see photo B88 below]. It took us an hour or so before Jim found one in the grasses along the roadside. Jim immediately sat down next to it and examined it very carefully. All of us gathered around to hear Jim's comments and to take our own photos. Jim is the author of *Field Guide to the Butterflies of North America*, and was our primary butterfly expert.

That evening after dinner we talked about that new butterfly which Jim had collected. We gathered around the table to hear Jim, Bonnie, and Johnna talk about the details of Johnna's discovery. It was a lively discussion and one that I enjoyed immensely.

Johnna, Bonnie and Jim Brock looking at Jobani Satyr

The following day found us back on Oso Creek. Bonnie drove us about four miles toward the headwaters, and the rest of us walked back along the creek. We found 47 butterfly species during our walk. Several of those were of special interest: Thicket Hairstreak, Rawson's Metalmark, Red-spotted Purple, Arizona Sister, Mourning Cloak, Canyonland Satyr, Desert Cloudywing, and Arizona and Golden Banded-Skippers.

The **Thicket Hairstreak** [see photo B89 below] was most special. Its deep reddish-brown color and white median band and a W near the outer angle, along with the lone short cell bar on the underside of the forewing, gave it distinctive appearance. Although it had been recorded in Big Bend, Big Bend's Chisos Mountains were actually visible that day from the Carmens, I had never found it there, and so it became one of my most favorite butterflies.

We spent the next morning walking down Canon Dos for a mile or more. It was another super butterfly-day. My list of species from that day included 41 species, of which several were outstanding. Those included Great Purple Hairstreak, Red-spotted Purple, Arizona Sister, Weidemeyer's Admiral, Canyonlands Satyr, Chisos Skipperling, both Chisos and Golden Banded-Skippers, Bronze Roadside-Skipper, and Acacia and Arizona Skippers.

Weidemeyer's Admiral (see photo B90 below) was a surprise. I had seen this large black and white butterfly in Arizona in the past, it does not occur within the Texas Big Bend region, and here it was in the Carmens. That represents a significant gap in its range. I wondered about the possibility of my Mexican Weidemeyer's Admiral being a new subspecies.

The other surprise in the Carmens was a **Chisos Skipperling** [see photo B91 below], a tiny skipper named after Big Bend's Chisos Mountains, but after so many, many hours of searching for butterflies in the Chisos without finding it, I found one in the Carmens. I couldn't help but wonder if the Chisos Skipperlings found in Big Bend were only a strays from the Carmens. This could also be the case for several other rare Chisos butterflies.

The next day, after another hearty breakfast, we left the lodge and drove down the mountain to Pilares, gave our thanks for a marvelous stay, and continued back into the desert. We drove to Musquiz for the night, staying at the Sabino Gordo Hotel.

In the morning, as we headed to the States, we stopped at the Rio Sabinas for part of the morning before continuing northward. We added nine trip butterflies there: Checkered and Great Southern Whites, Cloudless Sulphur, Fatal Metalmark, Phaon Crescent, Bordered Patch, Common Buckeye, Carolina Satyr, and Whirlabout. The Common Buckeye is common in the states, but it was new for our Maderas del Carmen trip. And it provided us with the final Mexican species. It had been a wonderful trip with some good friends, but seeing a Joboni Satyr was the trip highlight.

Short-tailed Skipper

Taxiles Skipper

Umber Skipper

Red Satyr

Jobani Satyr

Thicket Hairstreak

Weidermeyer's Admiral

Chisos Skipperling

Mexico Butterfly Trip, June 2007

A follow-up Maderas del Carmen trip, about a year after our May 2006 trip, was taken primarily due to our interest of learning more about the Jacobi Satyrs, a butterfly new to science. And so, Betty and I drove to Del Rio to join up with Eric and Sally Finkelstein; Jim Brock and Bob Behrstock arrived soon afterwards.

We left Del Rio in Eric's SUV on the morning of June 17 and, after a lunch stop in Musquiz, we arrived at Pilares at about 4pm. After a brief visit with Bonnie McKinney, manager of the Carmen Biosphere Reserve, we drove up into the Carmens to Campo Dos, where we stayed all three nights of our visit.

En route to Campo Dos, we stopped a few times to see what butterflies might be found along the roadside. By the time we reached our destination, I had recorded a dozen species, including Black, Eastern Tiger, and Two-tailed swallowtails. I had seen both Black and Two-tailed Swallowtail in the Carmen highlands on previous trips, but the **Eastern Tiger Swallowtail** [see photo B92 below] was new for me in the Carmens. It was easily identified from the wide black stripe and pinkish patch near the tail on the underside. Although this swallowtail is widespread throughout almost all of the eastern half of the United States, it is absent in the eastern portion of the Lower Rio Grande Valley. Its range continues, after a gap of about 100 miles, in Mexico's Sierra del Carmens.

Our accommodations at Campos Dos did not compare with the grandiose lodging at Campo Uno where we had stayed on our previous trip, but at least we had a place to sleep. And David Padilla was there as our cook again; we ate our meals in the "cook shack." Actually, Campo Dos is located at a higher elevation than Uno and the adjacent forest and stream provided very different butterfly habitats. The cinquefoil shrubs were in full bloom; they served as a butterfly magnet.

Canon Dos

The next day was spent searching for butterflies at Campos Dos, including a canyon that runs down into a heavily forested area. I recorded 66 species in and around Campos Dos that day. Highlight species included Two-tailed and Pipevine Swallowtails, Mourning Cloak, Weidemeyer's Admiral, Meridian and Pacuvius Duskywings, and three skipperlings: Chisos, Many-spotted, and Four-spotted skipperlings. Although all three have been recorded in the Chisos Mountains in Big Bend National Park, I did not see any of them there during my 6-year residency there. Two of the three – Many-spotted and Four-spotted Skipperlings - were lifers; a good start for another trip into the Carmens.

That first full day at Campo Dos produced 62 butterfly species, many of which I had previously found at Campo Uno. New trip species, however, included Tailed Orange; Arizona, Colorado, and Xami hairstreaks; Orange-crested Groundstreak, Mountain Greenstreak, Red-spotted Purple, Canyonland Satyr, Desert and Northern Cloudywings, Meridian and Pacuvius Duskywings, Chisos and Golden Banded-Skippers, Texas Powdered-Skipper, and Dotted and Nysa Roadside-Skippers.

Most exciting for me was seeing the **Orange-crested Groundstreak** [see photo B93 below] in Mexico. On August 27, 1991, I had discovered this bug in Big Bend National Park where it represented a new species for the park, for all of Texas, and the United States. That new Big Bend record was likely a stray from the Carmens. The only previous U.S. record was one that Chris Durden had photographed in Langtry, Texas years earlier. Now, I was able to see it in its natural habitat in Mexico.

We spent two more full-days at Campo Dos, wandering the valley and the mountains searching for butterflies we previously had not seen. Although I did not find any lifers, several were surprisingly common at Campo Dos. Those marked "common" in my field journal included Black Swallowtail, Dainty Sulphur, Sleepy Orange, Mexican Yellow, Checkered White, Arizona and Gray Hairstreaks, Spring Azure, Reakirt's Blue, Texan and Vesta Crescents, American Lady, Variegated Fritillary, Canyonland Satyr, Northern Cloudywing, Golden-headed Scallopwing, and Golden Banded-Skipper.

Finding an **Arizona Hairstreak** [see photo B94]was extra special. I had somehow missed finding this species on earlier Carmen trips and in places where they had previously been reported; those misses were now remedied. The Arizona Hairstreak is an unusual hairstreak, principally due to its pale green color with a pattern of orange lines which form a W near the outer angle. And this Arizona Hairstreak was a real beauty. Seldom have I been so enchanted!

The next day was a duplicate of the first, butterfly-wise. I did, however, add eight species to my trip list, and one of those was a true specialty, a **Gold-costa Skipper** [see photo B95 below]. The word "costa" refers to the leading edge of the forewing that, in the Gold-costa Skipper is gold or yellowish in the right light. That feature gives it a unique character. Its' larval foodplant is fern acacia.

There was one more species that impressed me – the **Juniper Hairstreak** [see photo B96 below] - and not in a positive way. The Carmen's Juniper Hairstreak was rather dull without the distinct white and red streaks against a green or reddish background I was so familiar with in Juniper Hairstreaks in Texas. Others found in the Carmens also were of the pale characteristic. Perhaps, another new species or subspecies?

After four days in the Maderas del Carmen, and recording 85 species of butterflies, we left the area and drove north to Musquiz. Eight miles before town we stopped at a stream to see what might be found. It was an excellent stop! I recorded 38 species there in a little over two hours. Although most had already been recorded on the trip, 13 were new trip bugs: Giant Swallowtail, Little Yellow, Dusky-blue Groundstreak, Fatal and Rounded Metalmarks,

Tawny Emperor, Broken Silverdrop, Two-barred Flasher, White-striped Longtail, Laviana and Turk's-cap White-Skippers, Celia's Roadside-Skipper, and Portrillo Skipper.

The most outstanding of those butterflies, because it was the brightest and most distinguished, was the **Two-barred Flasher** [see photo B97 below]. I had a difficult time photographing it because it was so active, flying out and back from one leafy perch to another. It reminded be of an Empidonax flycatcher further north.

Quatro Cienegas

We found accommodations for the night at a motel in Musquiz, and the next morning we drove to Quatro Cienegas where we acquired rooms at the Quatro Cienega, a very nice place with friendly people; they seemed to be very familiar with key sites in Quatro Cienegas. We stayed there for two night and ate at Docs nearby.

Although I recorded only 32 butterfly species at Quatro Cienegas, four were trip bugs: Ornythion Swallowtail, Mimosa Yellow, Elada Checkerspot, and Common Wood-Nymph. The **Common Wood-Nymph** [see photo B98 below] was a surprise. Jim, too, was surprised at the habitat it was using; we found it among the wetland vegetation at the edge of the pools. Jim collected two specimens and took several photographs. He questioned its species status, and suggested that it possibly might be a new species or certainly a new subspecies. My knowledge of Common Wood-Nymph is from finding it mostly in the woods and fields in the East and in the lower Rocky Mountains. But I had no knowledge of its presence in wetlands such as where we found it at Quatro Cienegas.

The overall terrain at Quatro Cienegas is desert-like with numerous cacti and yuccas that surround several deep, natural pools. The Quatro Cienegas Basin is an official nature reserve with inflowing streams, with no natural outflow. A number of artificial channels lead out of the area for nearby irrigation. According to Wikipedia, the Quatro Cienegas is "highly protected by government authorities. Recently, NASA stated that the Cuatro Ciénegas Basin could have strong links to discovering life on Mars since the adaptability of bioforms in the region is unique in the world."

There are approximately 150 different plants and animals endemic to the valley and its surrounding mountains. Among the many aquatic species in the Reserve are three endemic turtles, eight endemic fish, and several endemic crustaceans and gastropods, especially freshwater snails. I was surprised at a soft-shelled turtle that seemed as interested in us as we were in it.

Author at Quatro Cienegas

Several environmental conservation organizations, such as Pronature Noreste, are working to preserve the area. Quatro Cienegas certainly is unique and requires special protection!

We left Quatro Cienegas on our third day and drove to Musquiz for the night, and then on to Texas and home the following day. I had recorded 104 butterfly species during our trip, but two species – Orange-crested Groundstreak and Common Wood-Nymph – are most memorable.

Eastern Tiger Swallowtail

Four-spotted Skipperling

Orange-crested Groundstreak

Arizona Hairstreak

Gold-costa Skipper

Juniper Hairstreak

Two-barred Flasher

Common Wood-Nymph

Mexico Butterfly Trip – October 2007

This trip began in Mission, Texas, where I attended a NABA (North American Butterfly Association) meeting, titled "El Cielo Butterfly Festival." Betty and I stayed at the Alamo Inn in the small town of Alamo, close enough to participate in the meeting and its various field trips. Prior to the meeting we spent two days searching the Valley for whatever butterflies we could locate. The best sites included a new butterfly garden at Falcon State Park, several miles up-river, Santa Ana National Wildlife Refuge near Alamo, the NABA gardens, Rio Grande Valley State Park, and Llano Grande State Park. Our list of butterflies for those first two days included 85 species.

The highlight of those days, before going into Mexico, was a **Telea Hairstreak** [see photo B99 below] at Falcon State Park.That tiny deep green hairstreak was a lifer for me and for several friends who had heard about it. At least a dozen butterfliers, wherever they were in and around the Lower Rio Grande Valley, suddenly put in their appearance at Falcon's butterfly garden; cell phones are marvelous instruments!

An add-on to the El Cielo Butterfly Festival was a bus trip into Mexico to find butterflies; Kim Garwood was our leader. We entered Mexico from Reynosa where we obtained our visas, and a few hours later we stopped at El Tinieblo's Mescal Museum; next was the tiny town of La Morita. At each stop I spent my available time searching the areas for butterflies. By the time we reached Monte's Hotel Monte, where we stayed overnight, I had recorded 112 species, a surprisingly high number considering I had spent most of the time on a bus.

La Florida

The first full day in the field began at nearby La Florida, an area containing a beautiful pool and good streamside vegetation. The most impressive finds there included Creamy and Giant Whites, Clench's Greenstreak, Red-bordered and Walker's Metalmarks, Mexican Fritillary, Pale-banded Crescent, White and Banded Peacocks, Malachite, Mexican Bluewing, Red Rim, Silver Emperor, Brown and Zilpa Longtails, Two-barred Flasher, Glazed Pellicia; Hermit, Hoary, Variegated, and Violet-banded skippers; and Common Mellana.

The **White Peacock** [see photo 100 below], a butterfly I had seen in the Lower Rio Grande Valley, seemed a perfect fit for La Florida. It was abundant there; I counted over 100 individuals. The White Peacock is mostly all white, with wide orange borders and with black round postmedian spots. From my experiences elsewhere, I discovered that it sometimes joins others to colonize favorite wetland sites. It utilizes a wide variety of larval foodplants, ranging from lippia and ruellia to frog fruit.

The Zilpa Longtail was another impressive bug that I had recorded only a few times before; it is rare in the Lower Rio Grande Valley. This **Zilpa Longtail** [see photo B101 below] was extremely well marked and I took a dozen or more photos as it moved from vine to vine. Legume vines provide it with its larval foodplants.

That night we stayed in Gomez Farias, and the next day we drove the newly paved Ocampo-El Naranjo Road. It partially follows a stream that was accessible only now and again. The streamside vegetation was in full flower, and so we spent considerable time searching the area for butterflies. I recorded more than 75 species there of which 30 of those were trip butterflies.

The most welcome butterfly that day was a Dark Kite-Swallowtail perched in the water, and a Ruby-spotted Swallowtail perched nearby on streamside vegetation. The **Dark Kite-Swallowtail** [see photo B102 below] was a lifer, I had missed it on several earlier occasions. Now I was able to see it well, although it moved around much of the time. Besides its large size, I was impressed by its black-and-white upperside and extremely long, very thin tails. It reminded me of the Zebra Swallowtail, a species found throughout much of the southeastern United States.

All during the remainder of the day we spent wandering along the roadsides and streamsides. By late afternoon our group left the field and drove to Gomez Farias where we had overnight accommodations.

El Salto

The following morning found us at El Salto, an area with a fast-flowing stream and numerous ponds scattered below a series of waterfalls. I had spent several days at El Salto over the years and considered El Salto one of my most productive butterfly sites. On this day, in spite of a bus-load of folks scouring the area, I recorded more than 90 species; 62 were trip bugs and 10 were lifers. Seventeen of those were exclusive, found nowhere else on this trip. They included Lepida (Satyr) Eyemark, Cream-tipped and Quilted Metalmarks, Orion Cecropian, One-spotted Prepona, Angled and Morous Leafwings; Glacier-blue, Gold-stained, and Tailed Satyrs; Green Flasher, Obscure Bolla, Alana White-Skipper, and Crystal-winged, Nikko, Salenas, and Zygia (Black-dotted) skippers. Most of those were well-marked with unique patterns.

Perhaps, the most appealing of those bugs were the Quilted Metalmark and Crystal-winged Skipper. The **Quilted Metalmark** [see photo B104 below], was well-named. The upperside looked just like its name, with "quilted" panels on the forewings and with broad lighter margins containing black steaks. It wasn't a colorful bug but was attractive nonetheless.

In contrast, the **Chrystal-winged Skipper** [see photo B104 below], was pale with scattered light-blue panels, many edged with white, and orange-brown patches near the wingtips. This spread-wing skipper looked very different than the majority of spread-wing skippers. It truly is a tropical butterfly with a range which extends along most of the Gulf Coast.

We returned to Gomez Farias for the night, and the next morning, the bus took the Alta Cima Road above Gomez Farias to Los Troncones. We spent the morning hours there before heading north toward the States; our Mexico time was running out. However, Los Troncones produced about 125 butterfly species, resulting in the richest site we were able to visit by bus.

Butterfliers at Los Troncones

Although we spent only four hours at Los Troncones, my bus-mates spent their time running here and there searching for lifers. When any one of them found something which required help with identification, they would call for help and then everyone would hurry to see what it might be. Although most of what I recorded had already been found, there were six Los Troncones exceptions: Tailless Scrub-Hairstreak; Mexican-M, Red-spotted, Strophus (Blue-metal), and Zebrina hairstreaks; and Mountain (Brown-spotted) Greenstreak. I have always admired hairstreaks and the Red-spotted Hairstreak was my favorite.

I had an excellent view of the **Red-spotted Hairstreak** [see photo B105 below], a rather small, pale butterfly with an abundance of reddish median lines and basal spots. The upperside is deep blue in males and bluish-gray in females. Like all hairstreaks, getting a good photo took a while as I had to follow it around until it finally landed on a white flower and remained still.

Los Troncones also produced two metalmarks that were trip exclusives: Blue and Curve-winged Metalmarks. The Curve-wing was a lifer, but I had seen Blue Metalmarks on an earlier Mexico trip and it also occurs near Brownsville, Texas, in the Lower Rio Grande Valley. Its larval foodplants were unknown at the time, but we now know it is fern acacia, a low ground woody plant. Although Curve-winged Metalmarks lack the color and glamor of Blue Metalmarks, their shape and subtle colors give them a special appearance.

The **Curve-winged Metalmark** [see photo 105 below] unlike the Red-spotted Hairstreak, seemed actually to pose for me so I could take its picture. Because of its unique shape, unlike any of the other butterflies seen that day, it was readily identified. My Curve-winged Metalmark was a female, identified by the large pale spot on its leading edge; males are a darker overall color.

Other exclusives of note that day included Empress Leilia, Broad-tipped Clearwing, Sharp Banded-Skipper, Morning Glory Pellicia, and Obscure Bolla.

Reviewing my list of butterflies, afterwards, I discovered eleven truly special species that are not mentioned above. They include Red-spotted Swallowtail at several locations; Narrow-banded Dartwhite at several locations; Superb (Great or Debora) Cycadian at Gomez Farias; Regal Hairstreak at La Florida; Mountain (Brown-spotted) Greenstreak at Los Troncones; Chained Hairstreak along the Alta Cima Road; Red-flocked Ministreak at La Florida; Arcitus Swordtail along the Alta Cima Road; Carousing Metalmark at La Morita; Black-patched Metalmark along the Ocampo-El Naranjo Road; Red-bordered Pixie at La Florida; and Tiger Heliconian at La Florida,

Telea Hairstreak

white Peacock

Zilpa Longtail

Dark Kite-Swallowtail

Quilted Metalmark

Crystal-winged Skipper

Red-spotted Hairstreak

Curve-winged Metalmark

Mexico Butterfly Trip – February 2008

Betty and I drove to Del Rio, Texas, on February 8, where we met Eric and Sally Finkelstein. We ate dinner with them and stayed the night. The next day, with Eric driving his SUV, we crossed the border into Mexico and drove to Metahuala, San Luis Potosi. We ate dinner in Metahuala, and then drove on to Rio Verde for the night. We had driven 655 miles that day.

Early the next morning, we drove out to Media Luna Lake to see if the area might be a good site for butterflies. We quickly discovered that Media Luna Lake already was already crowded with local families, dashing our hopes of finding any butterflies of significance. We then drove back to the Rio Verde Hotel for breakfast and afterwards drove an hour and a half to Tamasopo. We acquired rooms at the Hotel Villa Ascension, and then drove out to the Pointe de Dios Falls.

Tamascopo is located at 1,200 feet elevation in the foothills of the Sierra Madre Oriental. The surrounding mountains rise to about 5,000 feet above sea level. Advertisements claim that Tamasopo is famous for its "enchanting waterfalls in a lush rain forest." The falls were not as spectacular as advertised, but the setting was within a lush environment.

Pointe de Dios Falls

In spite of people scattered here and there around the falls, I was able to find a few butterflies. The most significant of those was a **Plain Satyr** [see photo B107 below] a lifer that truly was a rather plain, grayish, little satyr that lived up its name. But a lifer, nonetheless.

The following day, we left Tamasopo and drove to Golendrina where we acquired rooms for the night at Hotel Vergal Huasteca. In the morning, we drove to Sotano de las Golondrinas, a famous landmark that I had looked forward to seeing for many years. And what a monument to nature it was! It is a huge limestone pit located within a rugged terrain. In Spanish, Golondrinas means "Basement of the Swallows," owing to the many birds which nest on the limestone walls. These birds, however, are White-collared Swifts, not swallows.

Sotano de las Golondrinas is a popular tourist attraction. Wikipedia describes it thusly:

> Each morning, flocks of birds exit the cave by flying in concentric circles, gaining height until they reach the entrance. In the evening a large flock of swifts circles the mouth of the cave and about once each minute, a group of perhaps 50 breaks off and heads straight down towards the opening. When they cross the edge, the birds pull in their wings and free-fall, extending their wings and pulling out of their dive when they reach their nests.

Eric and author at La Golondrinas

I was much impressed with the swifts and their behavior, but my principal interest in the area was finding butterflies. Searching the area, I recorded three dozen species of which Thoas Swallowtail, Ghost Yellow, Anna's Eighty-eight, Blomfild's Beauty; Angled, Pale-spotted, and Pointed leafwings; and Thick- tipped Greta were most interesting. However, the butterfly of the day was a **Splendid Mapwing** [see photo B108 below] that I found perched at the very edge of the pit; it was without equal. What an amazing creature! It not only was a lifer, but because of where I found it, will forever dominate my memory of Sotano de las Golandrinas.

The following day, after a quick resurvey of the Golandrinas area, we drove to Vicente and on to Tamtoc where I found very few butterflies, new or trip bugs. Maybe it was because I spent too much time examining the strange ruins at Tamtoc. Less than 200 acres in size, located on the northeast bank of the Tampaon River, it is considered to be one of the most important Huastecan urban centers of the last pre-Hispanic period. It lasted a few centuries but was suddenly abandoned in the 16th century, prior to the Spanish invasion.

Eric at Tomtoc ruins

One of the most unusual characteristics that distinguish Tamtoc is the remarkable feminine presence. To date, according to Wikipedia, 90% of the burials discovered there have been women. In addition, women are depicted in most of the clay and ceramic figurines found there; they are thought to have held a high rank in the social divisions of the community. An exception is illustrated in the photo above. One can't help but wonder why this particular ruin stands out and has been protected. Tomtoc produced only one butterfly of significance, a **Redundant Skipper** [see photo B110 below], a lifer. Its name does not fit into my understanding of redundancy. Except for one other sighting of the species at El Salto, I have never recorded it again. But, in spite of its boring appearance, it was a lifer.

In mid-afternoon, we drove to Xilitta where we acquired rooms in the El Castille, an historic hotel in downtown Xilitta. After checking in we walked to a nearby restaurant, that I no longer can recall its name, but we ate an excellent meal. And during our two-day stay in Xilita, I was very much impressed with the city, with the precariously steep streets, jungle-like gardens, and much greenery. I was told that it was the British eccentric Edward James who built the 80-acre jungle garden, complete with natural waterfalls and pools, known now as Las Pozas; his objective was to create a "Garden of Eden." It was Las Pozas that interested us most.

Las Pozas

We spent most of our field time searching for butterflies in and around Las Pozas. Although I was disappointed in the total numbers found, I did succeed in recording several species that satisfied my expectations. Most significant were Red-spotted Temmark, Temple Scinitellant, Gray-based and Square-tipped Crescents, Falcate Prepona, Turquoise Emperor, Hermes Satyr, and Salvin Ticlear [see photo B111 below], a butterfly very much like a clearwing. It flitted about among the vegetation, reminiscent of clearwings.

The **Square-tipped Crescent** (see photo B112 below] was also impressive. It possessed a wing pattern very much like most crescents, but its long wing gave it the appearance of heliconians and ticlears. Another lifer!

After two enjoyable days in and around Xilita, we drove ten miles to Trinadad, a village of about 400 inhabitants, and located in a shallow valley with adjacent highlands. We were told that the highlands contained an area of cloud forest, but we did not have time to investigate. We spent our time in the lowlands around the village of Trinidad, Queretaro.

Trinidad

During the short time spent in the Trinidad area, I photographed nine butterflies which I had forgotten about until I discovered them in my Mexican butterfly photo archives while preparing this document. Five of those were special: Black-painted Tile-White, Salome Yellow, Tailless Scrub-Hairstreak, Mexican Silverspot, and Pine Crescent.

The **Black-pointed Tile-White** [see photo B112 below] was not only a lifer, but one of the neatest little butterflies I have ever photographed. Notice that all of the black lines are either pointed or scraggly. The inner portion of its forewings also possesses a broad yellow patch. From one angle the outer pattern gave me the impression of birdwings.

By mid-afternoon it was time to move on. We drove to Jalpan, where we found rooms in the Hotel Maria del Carmen in downtown. Jalpan is known as the "Athens of Veracruz" because of the strong cultural influence of its university, Universidad Veracruzana, the main public university in the State of Veracruz.

It was too late in the day to spend time searching for butterflies, so we ate an early dinner at the hotel and then walked around town for a couple of hours. It appeared to be a clean and busy city; I was impressed!

In the morning. we spent only a couple hours searching the Jalpan area for butterflies. Of the two dozen species I recorded, two were lifers: Dusky Sombermark and Ardent Crescent. The two species showed considerable contrast in their pattern and color. The **Dusky Sombermark** [see photo B113 below] was a somber color with a central dark patch and dark basal markings, and its banded antennae contained red clubs.

Ardent Crescent [see photo B114 below] was colorful and much more energetic. And it looked much more like the crescents commonly seen in the United States.

That afternoon, we drove on to Sierra Gorda. Located at 4,600 feet elevation, the area has a reputation for having the most diverse ecosystem in Mexico, containing the largest number of plants and animals in the country. We soon discovered that the Sierra Gorda also offered superb butterfly habitats, some of which were new on our journey.

Much of the Sierra Gorda region, which extends into the Mexican state of Guanajuato, was declared a biosphere reserve in 2007, an international program to preserve biodiversity. Although ecotourism occurs throughout the region, research activities, traditional economic activities, and low impact development, are allowed.

We obtained rooms at the nearby San Juan Los Doran B&B operated by Margarita Pedraga, a lovely lady who was very knowledgeable about the area, including the resident butterflies. Sierra Gorda proved to be one of our most productive butterfly stops.

Author at Sierra Gorda

During the day and a half spent searching Sierra Gorda, I recorded more than 100 species of butterflies, of which Surprising White, Great-veined and Large Hairstreaks, Somber Bluewing, Pine and Square-tipped Crescent, Orange-striped Eight-eight, One-spotted Prepona, Renata's Satyr, Bell's Scallopwing, Black- patched Duskywing, Broken Silverdrop, Mexican Sandy-Skipper, and Chalk – marked Skippers were all lifers. What a huge number of Mexican specialties! The largest number of lifers found anywhere on the trip.

It is difficult to select one of the Sierra Gorda butterflies to illustrate. But in reviewing my photographs, one stands out as most colorful and special, Surprising White. The **Surprising White** [see photo B115 below] was truly a surprise. It was a large all-black butterfly with a broad red patch on the inner-side of the hindwing, not at all like the majority of whites.

In the afternoon, we drove to the nearby Rio Jalpan to see what butterflies might occur there, but we returned to Magarita's B&B for the night. Rio Jalpan produced several trip bugs but only one lifer, the **Orange-striped Eighty-eight** [see photo B116 below] another surprise. Until the day I found this gorgeous bug near the Rio Jalpan, I had not known of its existence; I guess I assumed that there could be only be one eighty-eight, Anna's Eighty-eight. Finding new and unexpected species is what makes trips like this one so enduring.

The following day, we drove to the town of Rio Verde and on to Ayatla, in the state of Queretaro, and then on through Matehuala to Real del Catorce where we found rooms at Meson de la Abundance. It was a long day and we were unable to spent time searching for butterflies.

The next day we headed for home. We ate a chicken lunch, purchased from a roadside booth, and we were back in Del Rio, Texas, by 8pm.

I had listed a total of 205 butterfly species on the trip, and 14 of those were lifers: Three-tailed Swallowtail, Black-pointed White, Surprising White, Black-veined Hairstreak, Large Groundstreak, Shining Greenstreak, Ardent Crescent, Godman's Mapwing, Orange-striped Eighty-eight, Renanta's and Terrestrial Satyrs, Dark Cloudywing, and Chalk-marked and Gold-washed Skippers.

Plain Satyr

Splendid Mapwing

Redundant Skipper

Salvin's Ticlear

Square-tailed Crescent

Black-pointed Title-White

Dusky Somberwing

Ardent Crescent

Surpising White

Orange-striped Eighty-eight

Mexico Butterfly Trip – October 2008

Betty and I drove to Del Rio, Texas to meet up with Eric and Sally Finkelstein. We stayed overnight with the Finkelsteins and early the next day (Oct. 20), with Eric driving his SUV, we crossed into Mexico at Pharr. We drove in the rain all the way to Tuxpan, Veracruz, about 550 miles. That evening we found accommodations at the La Posada. Although it had no hot water; we did eat a decent meal.

It was still raining in the morning, although it cleared by noon. We drove to Quiahuaztlan where we spent a couple hours butterflying. I recorded 49 species there, of which five were lifers: Carousing Jewelmark, Simple Patch, Crinkled Banner, White-crescent Longtail, and Malicious Skipper. I was most impressed by the colorful **Crinkled Banner** [see photo B118 below]. It did look crinkled. And it took me considerable time to obtain a decent photograph to show its crinkled appearance. In the meantime, I watched it flying from one leaf to another before it finally settled down.

Quialuiztlan, meaning "place in rain" in Nahuatl, is one of many sites in Mexico containing ruins with semi-natural habitat surrounding the managed grounds. Quiahuiztlan is one of the Toltec's most beautiful sites. It is located on the Veracruz coast very close to where Hernan Cortez and his small army landed in the New World in 1519. The ruins themselves were occupied since the 16th century as part of the Totonac culture. Some of the ruins - the temples, ballcourt, plazas and residences - have been at least partly restored.

Quialuiztlan

Although the archeological site covers a reasonably small acreage, it was built on a ridge above the coastal plain with defensive works that utilized high terraced walls. It seemed highly effective. The grounds contained at least a dozen cemeteries that consisted of small mausoleums in the form of small temples.

We spent a couple hours there searching the grounds and surrounding vegetation for butterflies. I listed only 29 species, but eight were special: Green-eyed White, Common Melwhite, Barred Yellow, Carousing Jewelmark, Tropical Buckeye, Spot-banded Sister, Yellow-tipped Flasher, and Dusted Spurwing.

The **Carousing Jewelmark** [see photo B118 below] made my day! What an exquisite little metalmark! About the size of a quarter when perched, its undersides possessed a wild combination of colors, from rust with blue spots, red outer borders, yellowish forewing edges, and white bars, and with a reddish head. Although I had never recorded it before, its range extends down the Gulf Coast and all of the Yucutan.

That afternoon we drove to Cardel, Mexico's famous hawk-watch site. Millions of migrating of raptors pass over the area in spring and fall. We wandered about the hawk-watch grounds for a couple hours before obtaining accommodations for the night at the Hotel Benevento.

In the morning, after again searching for butterflies on the hawk-watch grounds, and finding no lifers, we drove on toward Jalapa. We stopped to butterfly at Chichicaxtle, Mexico's secondary, a more inland hawk-watch site. Except for an Ornython Swallowtail and a Sleepy Orange, we found no new trip bugs there.

Our next stop was at Cerro Gordo, a rather arid area where we walked along a long lane through open fields to where the track dropped into a deep canyon; we walking only about half-a-mile into the canyon but did not have time to go any further. But the canyon undoubtedly would have been a worthwhile place for butterflies

Cerro Gordo area

Cerro Gordo, in general, proved to be a superb area for butterflies; my list included 40 species. Eleven of those were not found elsewhere else on the trip: Broad-banded Swallowtail, Temple Scinitllant, Broken Silverdop, Karwinski Beauty, Hewitson's and Long-tailed Agunas, Melon Mottled-Skipper, Bell's Scallopwing, Jalapas Cloudywing, Erichson's White-Skipper, and Megalops Skipper.

Karwinski Beauty [see photo B119 below] was a remarkable butterfly with the underside covered with a mass of scraggly lines, two eyespots, a gold bar on the forewings, and dark antennae with noticeably black clubs. The upperside, although seldom seen, is the most colorful: gold-orange with all-black wingtips with three pale spots. Eight other Beauties occur in Mexico, and they all possess amazing orange and black patterns.

In late afternoon we drove on to Xico for the night. We stayed at Hotel Coyopolan and discovered it had a very good restaurant; it proved to be our best overnight on our trip. It also provided a central location for visits to Chavarrillo and Estanzuela. On our visit to Estanzuela, we began at a wooded area above a soccer field where we ate lunch we bought in town.

Estanzuela produced 28 butterfly species; seven were exclusives, found nowhere else on the trip: De la Maza's Mimic-White, Rayed Sister, Confused Satyr, Gold-tufted Skipper, Dardarina Skipperling, and Band-spotted and Freeman's Skippers. Of those seven species, **Rayed Sister** [see photo B121 below] was most appealing, with its all-black upperside except for a broad golden band across each wing. The underside was strongly rayed with gold-and-black bands, and on a closer look, I could see tiny white spots on the forward edge of the wing. Rayed Sister is truly an outstanding butterfly.

Chavarrillo

At Chavarrillo, we walked along railroad tracks at the edge of town for about three hours; the wooded edges looked promising. I recorded 32 butterfly species there. Eight were trip exclusives: Broad-banded and Thoas Swallowtails, Gold-banded Hairstreak, American Lady, Whitened Bluewing, Two-banded Flasher, Klug's Clearwing, and Guatamalan Cracker. Two of the eight – Broad-banded Swallowtail and Klug's Clearwing – were lifers!

I was particularly interested in the **Klug's Clearwing** [see photo B121 below]. It was not the typical clearwing with see-through wing panels; it was more similar to heliconians. The underside of the hindwings was a clear pale orange with black borders, with oblong white spots. It was fascinating nevertheless.

Sometimes, some of the most sterile-looking sites can hold amazing finds. I recorded some really unusual bugs along that railroad right-of-way: Green-eyed White, Barred yellow, Tailed Orange, Isabella's and Julia Heliconians, Malachite, Mexican Fritillary, Whitened Bluewing, Mexican Cycadian, Orange Mapwing, Rusty-tipped Page, Guatamalan Cracker, Two-barred Flasher, Dorantes Longtail, and Mazans Scallopwing.

The **Orange Mapwing** [see photo B122 below] was my favorite! What a gorgeous creature, mostly orange with a black bar below the black and orange-spotted wingtips and, on a close look, was a pair of short, stubby tails. The underside lacked the bright orange color, but was dominated by a spiderweb like pattern. Perhaps, that is where the mapwing name originated.

Texola Falls

Afterwards, on our route to our overnight in Xico, we visited nearby Texola Falls, an area with considerable natural habitats. Although the falls itself was worth a visit, the area was busy with locals and tourists. In spite of the traffic, I did record five species not found elsewhere on our trip. Costa-spotted Mimic-White, Black Hairstreak, Orange-patched Crescent, Guatemalan Patch, and Spot-banded Longtail.

The **Orange-patched Crescent** [see photo B123 below] reminded me so much of several look-alike crescents in the states, but none of those are as bright and flashy. Considering all of the butterflies recorded on this trip, it was one of my favorites.

We didn't stay long at Texola Falls, but continued on to Xico where we stayed the night at Hotel Coyopolan and enjoyed a very good dinner. In the morning we returned to Chavarrillo for a couple hours where we again walked along the railroad tracks in search of butterflies. Both sides of the right-of-way were filled with flowering shrubs and vines.

Within a few hours at Chavarrillo, I recorded eleven additional specialties. They included Tiger Mimic-White; Burnt-chocolate, Pearly, and Sky-blue hairstreaks; Leilia's Clearwing, both Blomfild's and Karwinski's Beauties, Simple Checkerspot, Orange-patched Crescent, Tiger Leafwing, and Gold-washed Skipper.

The **Tiger Mimic-White** [see photo B124 below] was one of the most unusual butterflies I found in all of Mexico. It reminded me of clearwings in shape and behavior. It flitted here and there until it finally perched on a leaf. I was unsure what I had found. Although its behavior was clearwing-like, its appearance was more in line with heliconians. Its name seemed most appropriate.

In early afternoon, we continued on to Finca Hilde El Mirador where we had reservations. El Mirador, located near Totutla, Veracruz, is a 4,200-acre private coffee plantation/preserve containing good native forest. We stayed in Jorge Muller's guest house, and his cook prepared food for us at breakfast, lunch, and dinner. It truly was a pleasant two-day stay. Jorge was a most gracious host!

El Mirador

Jorge guided us to three super locations, all within five miles of his house. And the butterflies we found there were extraordinary! Perhaps, our best butterflies there included an **Imperial Arcus** [see photo B125 below] a green, gold and black hairstreak, and hundreds of **Anna's Eighty-eights** [see photo B126 below] that we found feeding on fallen fruit as we walked down the roadway; they swirled around me like cottonwood seeds.

We also had super views of Jethy's Mimic-White, Meton Hairstreak, Wavy-lined Sunstreak, Cloaked Scintillant, Bumblebee Metalmark, Banner Metalmark, Salvin's Clearwing, White-spotted Greta, Darkened Rusty Clearwing, Banded and Aliphera Longwings, East-Mexican and Blue-frosted Banners, Orange and Red Crackers, Curcumducta Satyr, Tawny Mottled-Skipper, Two-spotted Banded-Skipper, Mexican Sandy-Skipper, and Bottom-spotted and Red-studded Skippers.

Two of the smaller butterflies stood out as special: Wavy-lined Sunstreak and Red-studded Skipper. The **Wavy-lined Sunstreak** [see photo B127 below] is a hairstreak with long, filament-like tails. Although it was in constant motion, I had the impression that it was waving to me to say "I'm special." It truly was!

The **Red-studded Skipper** [see photo B127 below] is blended in extremely well with the background vegetation; it was difficult to get a clear view until it flew onto a nearby white Senecio. It wasn't until I got a close-up view before I could see the tiny red spots on the mottled, purplish upperside.

The next day was rainy and so we left El Mirador and drove down to Colonial Barrios, another Muller property, and out of the rain. We added four trip butterflies there: Yojoa Scrub-Hairstreak, Asine Longtail, Yellow-haired Pyramid-Skipper, and Many-banded Skipper. The **Yellow-haired Pyramid-Skipper** [see photo B129 below] is well-named because because of its "yellow-haired" name. It took a while to take a photo which could actually show its yellowish hairs. And sure enough, in the right light the yellowish hairs were obvious.

Tlacotalpan

After spending a few hours at Colonial Barrios, we drove on to Tlacotalpan for the night and found accommodations at the Tlacotalpan Hotel. Located in southern Veracruz along the Gulf, it is drained by the San Juan and Tuxpan Rivers. It was one of the few large Mexican cities where we stayed overnight that impressed me. The city of about 13,500 residents was clean. The buildings, especially the huge cathedral at the end of the street from our hotel, was beautiful. The city appeared well organized. After eating our meal at the hotel, we walked to the cathedral to admire it and the surrounding buildings. It was a relaxing and fascinating stay.

We left Tlacotalpan the following morning and drove to Tutla. After a couple hours butterflying the Tutla area, with little results, we drove on to Ruiz Cortina where we ate lunch in town and afterwards spent a couple hours looking for butterflies in nearby fields. I listed only two species: Barred Yellow and Mexican Dartwhite.

Our next destination was Catemaco where I had visited on several earlier occasions while searching for birds. But our butterflying that day was cut short due to rainy weather. So, we returned to Ruiz Cortina where we had lunch at the Bien Veneto; an excellent fish dinner. That afternoon was still cold and rainy, so we drove to Catemaco and the Los Arcos Hotel for the night.

Catemaco is located just off Highway 180, the main highway along the Gulf of Mexico between the cities of Veracruz and Villahermosa. The town of Catemaco is located on the north shore of Laguna de Catemaco, a freshwater lake about ten miles long, and the center of a fishing industry.

Catemaco

In the morning, with clearing weather, we drove in the rain to Montepio, at the end of the road. When heading back to Catemaco, we ran into clearing skies. Taking advantage of the warming afternoon, we spent a few hours in and around the Los Tuxtlas biological field station. It was there where we discovered the Darwin Trail which required permission to visit. After receiving permission from the local scientists, we walked the trail.

The trail was slick from recent rains, so we were forced to walk much slower than normal as we carefully followed the narrow path through the tropical greenery. The overcast sky added to the dim light which blended with the dense undergrowth. Even the birdlife seemed to be on hold, although an occasional call note was evident somewhere above.

A Zebra Heliconian lifted off from a perch as we passed, and an Isabella's Heliconian fluttered away through the mist. I had a distant view of a clearwing off to the right. Then suddenly Eric discovered a much smaller dark brown butterfly perched on a green leaf at knee-height that I had walked right by. We immediately zeroed in to identify this little bug. But it took several minutes before we could see the rusty underside and two black eyespots and the turquoise band across the partially open upper side. A **Turquoise-eyed**

Metalmark [see photo B129 below], a new species for all four of us. It was an exquisite creature that forever more will remind me of that unique site on the Darwin Trail.

And so it went the remainder of the day. And in spite of the rainy weather, I recorded a total of 88 species, including nine additional lifers: Black-edged Calehelis, Hewitson's Metalmark, Turquoise Emperor, Small Beauty, Northern Eyed-Skipper, and Suffused, Saliana, Inculta, and Alumna skippers.

The **Small Beauty** (see photo B130 below) was indeed a little beauty. Although the upperside is a small version of a Banded Peacock, the underside, as shown in my photo, is a mixture of narrow black-and-white lines, a broad white central band, a white diagonal band, and a thickened black band near the edge of the outer wing.

We left Catemaco the following day, heading back to Texas and home. We drove to Valle National that day where we found accommodations that night at the Vallereal Hotel. After securing rooms, we spent the remainder of the afternoon above town walking along a road under construction and in adjacent fields. All the butterflies found were repeats of those already recorded.

We left Valle National early the next morning and drove to Esperanza where we again attempted to butterfly above town in the cloud forest. But once again the weather did not agree, so we drove on to Cardel for the night. We left Cardel early the next morning for Zempoala where we had our first good butterflies in three days.

The Zempoala fields were filled with wildflowers, and the adjacent shrubbery was rich with butterflies. The most exciting species included Thoas Swallowtail, Golden Melwhite, Apricot Sulphur, Bold Mimic-White, Sky-blue Greatstreak, and Disturbed Tigerwing. All but the swallowtail were lifers.

The **Disturbed Tigerwing** [see photo B132 below] was my was my favorite. It looked a lot like an Isabella's Heliconian, but the underside showed broader vertical yellow bars, wavy bands across the forewings and a single yellow band, encompassed in black on the forewing, and the black margin contained small white spots.

We spent our last overnight near Tampico, and the next morning we drove 300 miles to Texas, reaching Alamo by 5pm. It had been a marvelous trip, with finding 305 butterfly species; 63 of those were lifers!

Veracruz not only contains a rich biological diversity, but an amazing history which blends together with the natural resources. And the state's special natural and culture features are readily accessible.

Crinkled Banner

Carousing Jewelmark

Rayed Sister

Klug's Clearwing

Orange Mapwing;

Orange-patched Crescent

Tiger Mimic-White

Anna's 88

Wavy-lined Sunstreak

Red-studded Skipper

Yellow-haired Pyramid-Skipper;

References

Brock, Jim P., and Kenn Kaufman. 2003. Field Guide to Butterflies of North America. Boston, Mass., Houghton Mifflin Co.

Glassberg, Jeffrey. 2007. A Swift Guide to the Butterflies of Mexico and Central America. New York: Sunstreak Books, Inc.

Wauer, Roland H. 1999. Naturalist's Mexico. College Station, Texas A&M University Press.

_____ 2004. Butterflies of the Lower Rio Grande Valley. Boulder, Colorado: Johnson Books.

Printed in the United States
by Baker & Taylor Publisher Services